FORCE

Force

A FUNDAMENTAL CONCEPT OF AESTHETIC ANTHROPOLOGY

Christoph Menke

Translated by Gerrit Jackson

Fordham University Press

NEW YORK ‡ 2013

Copyright © 2013 Fordham University Press

This work was originally published as *Kraft: Ein Grundbegriff
äesthetischer Anthropologie*, © Suhrkamp Verlag Frankfurt am Main
2008. All rights reserved and controlled through Suhrkamp Verlag
Berlin.

Fordham University Press also publishes its books in a variety of
electronic formats. Some content that appears in print may not be
available in electronic books.

Library of Congress Cataloging-in-Publication Data is available
from the publisher.

Printed and bound in Great Britain by
Marston Book Services Ltd, Oxfordshire

15 14 13   5 4 3 2 1
First edition

CONTENTS

ABBREVIATIONS

REFERENCES IN PARENTHESES IN the text refer to the last cited source. For some sources, I have supplied alternative locators such as section or paragraph numbers as well as, after a semicolon, page numbers. The following abbreviations refer to frequently cited sources:

Aesthetics: Alexander Gottlieb Baumgarten, *Aesthetica—Ästhetik*, ed. and German trans. Dagmar Mirbach. Hamburg: Meiner, 2007.

"Baumgarten": Johann Gottfried Herder, "Begründung einer Ästhetik in der Auseinandersetzung mit Alexander Gottlieb Baumgarten" ("Foundations for an Aesthetics in Critical Engagement with Alexander Gottlieb Baumgarten"), in *Werke*, vol. 1, *Frühe Schriften 1764–1772*, ed. Ulrich Gaier. Frankfurt am Main: Deutscher Klassiker Verlag, 1985, 651–94.

BGE: Friedrich Nietzsche, *Beyond Good and Evil: Prelude to a Philosophy of the Future*, trans. Judith Norman. Cambridge: Cambridge University Press, 2002.

BT: Friedrich Nietzsche, *The Birth of Tragedy and Other Writings*, trans. Ronald Speirs. Cambridge: Cambridge University Press, 1999.

CJ: Immanuel Kant, *Critique of Judgment*, trans. Werner S. Pluhar. Indianapolis: Hackett, 1987.

Cognition: Johann Gottfried Herder, *On the Cognition and Sensation of the Human Soul: Observations and Dreams*, in *Philosophical Writings*, trans. Michael N. Forster. Cambridge: Cambridge University Press, 2002.

Daybreak: Friedrich Nietzsche, *Daybreak: Thoughts on the Prejudices of Morality*, trans. R. J. Hollingdale. Cambridge: Cambridge University Press, 1997.

Discipline: Michel Foucault, *Discipline and Punish: The Birth of the Prison*, trans. Alan Sheridan. New York: Vintage, 1979.

Discourse: René Descartes, *Discours de la méthode pour bien conduire sa raison, et chercher la vérité dans les sciences—Discourse on the Method*, in *The Philosophical Writings of René Descartes*, trans. John Cottingham, Robert Stoothoff, and Dugald Murdoch, 2 vols. Cambridge: Cambridge University Press, 1984–85, vol. 1, 111–51.

"Energie": Johann Georg Sulzer, "Von der Kraft (Energie) in den Werken der schönen Künste," in *Vermischte philosophische Schriften*. Leipzig: Weidmann und Reich, 1773; repr. Hildesheim: Olms, 1974.

Enquiry: Edmund Burke, *A Philosophical Enquiry into the Origin of Our Ideas of the Sublime and Beautiful*, ed. Adam Phillips. Oxford: Oxford University Press, 1990.

"Fourth Grove": Johann Gottfried Herder, "Critical Forests, or Reflections on the Art and Science of the Beautiful: Fourth Grove, On Riedel's *Theory of the Beaux Arts*," in *Selected Writings on Aesthetics*, trans. Gregory Moore. Princeton, N.J.: Princeton University Press, 2006, 199.

Fragments, 1880: Friedrich Nietzsche, "Nachgelassene Fragmente" of Early 1880, in *Kritische Studienausgabe*, ed. Giorgio Colli and Mazzino Montinari. Munich: Deutscher Taschenbuch/de Gruyter 1988, vol. 9, 9–33.

GS: Friedrich Nietzsche, *The Gay Science: With a Prelude in German Rhymes and an Appendix of Songs*, trans. Josefine Nauckhoff. Cambridge: Cambridge University Press, 2001.

"Landschaft": Joachim Ritter, "Landschaft: Zur Funktion des Ästhetischen in der modernen Gesellschaft," in Ritter, *Subjektivität*. Frankfurt am Main: Suhrkamp, 1974, 141–64.

Meditations: René Descartes, *Meditationes de prima philosophia—Meditations on First Philosophy*, in *The Philosophical Writings of René Descartes*, trans. John Cottingham, Robert Stoothoff, and Dugald Murdoch, 2 vols. Cambridge: Cambridge University Press, 1984–85, vol. 2, 3–62.

Monadology: G. W. Leibniz, *Monadology*, ed. Nicholas Rescher. Pittsburgh: University of Pittsburgh Press, 1991.

"Monument": Johann Gottfried Herder, "A Monument to Baumgarten," in *Selected Writings on Aesthetics*, trans. Gregory Moore. Princeton, N.J.: Princeton University Press, 2006, 41–50.

Nietzsche: Martin Heidegger, *Nietzsche*, vol. 1, *The Will to Power as Art*, trans. David Farrell Krell. London: Routledge, 1981, and vol. 4, *Nihilism*, trans. Frank A. Capuzzi. San Francisco: Harper and Row, 1982.

Poetry: Alexander Gottlieb Baumgarten, *Reflections on Poetry—Meditationes philosophicae de nonnullis ad poema pertinentibus*, trans. Karl Aschenbrenner. Berkeley: University of California Press, 1954.

"Rhapsody": Moses Mendelssohn, "Rhapsody or Additions to the Letters on Sentiments," in *Philosophical Writings*, trans. Daniel O. Dahlstrom. Cambridge: Cambridge University Press, 1997, 131–68.

RRUM: Friedrich Nietzsche, "Reconnaissance Raids of an Untimely Man," in *TI*, 43–75.

Rules: René Descartes, *Regulae ad directionem ingenii—Rules for the Direction of the Mind*, in *The Philosophical Writings of René Descartes*, trans. John Cottingham, Robert Stoothoff, and Dugald Murdoch, 2 vols. Cambridge: Cambridge University Press, 1984–85, vol. 1, 7–78.

TI: Friedrich Nietzsche, *Twilight of the Idols: Or How to Philosophize with a Hammer*, trans. Duncan Large. Oxford: Oxford University Press, 1998.

PREFACE

WHY AESTHETICS? THE ANSWER seems obvious: aesthetics exists—and is, in fact, necessary—because the aesthetic exists. It exists because there are objects—such as music, art, architecture, design, fashion, ballet, athletic competition—which we designate as sublime or beautiful and which lend themselves to philosophical reflection. Because there are aesthetic objects, there must be an aesthetic theory that accounts for them. Thus aesthetics must take its rightful place among the other subdisciplines of philosophy, namely, political philosophy, ethics, philosophy of science, and philosophy of culture.

Nonetheless, can it not be argued that what we call "art"—such as design, fashion, even athletics—is merely another part of the economy, of the so-called culture industry? Or that what we call "beautiful" is merely a trigger for pleasurable sensations in the brain? Is it even obvious that these objects form a coherent domain that can be called "aesthetic"? Are they not just a group of very different entities? It seems that we must already be convinced of the existence of aesthetic objects and interested in them in order to "do" aesthetics. If we answer the question "Why study aesthetics?" by naming the discipline's objects, then does aesthetics not merely become the expression of a personal interest whose reputation will rise (or fall) as this interest waxes (or wanes)?

But aesthetic objects (and our interest in them) are not what make up aesthetics. It is, rather, aesthetics that makes up the domain of aesthetic objects. Aesthetics constitutes the theory of the aesthetic only because it defines a thing as an "aesthetic" object in the first place. We cannot answer the question "Why be concerned with aesthetics?" with the response "Because the aesthetic exists." The question really means, *Why be concerned with the aesthetic?* What does it mean, and what are the preconditions and the consequences of the fact that aesthetics makes up "the aesthetic"—and hence itself?

———

WHAT FOLLOWS WILL REVISIT the role played by aesthetics by way of a retelling, that is, a retelling of the "birth" of aesthetics in the eighteenth century, in the period between Baumgarten's *Aesthetics* and Kant's *Critique of Judgment*. We will see that aesthetics did not expand the range of the legitimate objects of philosophical inquiry. All of these objects existed before aesthetics. Rather, by introducing the category of "the aesthetic," aesthetics fundamentally redefined these objects. Most important, this account of the historical genesis of aesthetics will show that the introduction of the category of the "aesthetic" required nothing less than a transformation of the fundamental terms of philosophy. The beginning of aesthetics is, in fact, the beginning of modern philosophy.

It is aesthetics, then, and more precisely Baumgarten's *Aesthetics*, that shaped the concept of the subject: as the agent defined by the totality of his faculties and capacities. By conceiving sensible cognition and representation as the exercise of subjective faculties that are acquired in practice, Baumgarten framed the modern conception of human practices. In doing this, he also framed philosophy as the inquiry into the conditions that enable the success of these practices. *That* is the reason that aesthetics—defined as the reflection upon the aesthetic—is a central pillar of modern philosophy. In aesthetics, the philosophy of the subject or of the subject's faculties assures itself of its own possibility.

Yet here, in the aesthetic and the reflection on it, the philosophy of the subject also meets its most determined opponent, one who attacks it from the inside. For the aesthetics "in the Baumgartian manner" (Herder), taken as the theory of the sensible faculties of the subject, faces a different aesthetics, namely, the aesthetics of force. This alternative conception sees the aesthetic not as a study of sensible cognition and representation but as a play of expression—propelled by a force that, rather than being exercised like a faculty in practices, realizes *itself*. This force does not recognize or represent anything because it is "obscure" and unconscious; this is not a force of the subject but of the human, as distinct from the subject. The aesthetics of force is a science of the nature of humans—of their aesthetic nature as distinct from the culture, acquired by practice, of their practices.

———————

THAT IS THE HYPOTHESIS I intend to defend in the six chapters of this book. The first chapter, analyzing the rationalist concept of the sensible, recollects the point of departure of aesthetics: the sensible is that which is without determinable definition or measure. The second chapter reconstructs Baumgarten's aesthetics of sensible cognition as a theory of the subject and its faculties. This entails the controversy over whether aesthetic subjectivation should be interpreted as individualizing or as disciplining. The third and fourth chapters draw on writings by Herder, Sulzer, and Mendelssohn to develop the basic motifs of a countermodel, an aesthetics of force. This encompasses the aesthetic, understood as the operation of an "obscure" force, as a performance without generality, divorced from all norm, law, and purpose—a play. And the aesthetic, understood as the pleasure of self-reflection, is a process of the transformation of the subject and its faculties and practices—a process of aestheticization.

The aesthetics of force founds an anthropology of difference: between force and faculty, between human and subject. The two concluding chapters explore the consequences of this position: for the idea of philosophical aesthetics and for ethics as the theory of the good. More specifically, the fifth chapter turns to Kant to show that an aesthetics conceived as an aesthetics of force is a scene of an irresolvable contention between philosophy and aesthetic experience. The sixth chapter draws on Nietzsche to demonstrate the ethical importance of aesthetic experience as the play of force, which teaches us to distinguish between action and life.

———————

A NOTE ABOUT THE use of gendered pronouns in the text: In the German language, there is often no gender-neutral way to refer to an anonymous person; specifically, the German word for "human being" is grammatically masculine. In light of this fact as well as the gendered pronouns in most of the texts quoted in the book, Gerrit and I agreed that it was best to keep the language of the original text rather than compromise the brevity and fluidity of the language.

I want to thank Gerrit Jackson for his precise, meticulous translation and Katherine Ross for her patient and creative editorial work on the manuscript.

In the aesthetic condition, then, man is a *cipher* . . .

FRIEDRICH SCHILLER

CHAPTER ONE

Sensibility: The Indeterminacy of the Imagination

THE HISTORY OF AESTHETICS begins with an act of repudiation: a repudiation of the notion that there can be a theory about or a positive knowledge of the beautiful. Aesthetics begins with Descartes's doubt about its possibility. He writes to Marin Mersenne:

> You ask whether one can discover the essence [*la raison*] of beauty. This is the same as your earlier question—why [is] one sound . . . more pleasant than another—except that the word "beauty" seems to have a special relation to the sense of sight. But, in general, "beautiful" and "pleasant" signify simply a relation between our judgment and an object; and because the judgments of men differ so much from [one another], neither beauty nor pleasantness can be said to have any definite measure.[1]

Because the beautiful has no unifying essence [*raison*], because it is essentially without reason, it cannot be conceptualized. According "to some men's fancy [*phantasie*], [a flower bed] with three shapes will be the most beautiful; to others it will be one with four or five and so on. But whatever will please most men could be called the most beautiful without qualification; but what this is cannot be determined [*ce qui ne saurait être déterminé*]" (ibid.). The beautiful is the indeterminable.

THE CAPRICIOUSNESS OF THE SENSES

Descartes's definition of the beautiful as the indeterminable involves two moves that are essential to the idea of aesthetics. The first move consists in locating the beautiful in the domain of the senses. Descartes claims that the beautiful is an effect of its ability to produce a sensuous feeling in the subject, and therefore he identifies it with something agreeable. This fact makes all distinctions secondary. Thus there is no fundamental difference between a beautiful object that is created by nature and one that is made by humans, which we call "art." Nor is there is an essential difference between the person who produces a beautiful object and the person who sees it, nor between the act of making the beautiful object and the act of perceiving it. They are all one. In the same way, Descartes believes that it makes no fundamental difference whether he uses natural phenomena[2] or artificial arrangements[3] of colors and sounds to illustrate the play of varying impressions made by the beautiful. Nor, hence, does it make a fundamental difference whether we consider the genesis of the impression of beauty from the side of its production in works or from that of its reproduction in judgments. The reduction of the beautiful to that which produces a sensible effect unites in one domain what had, until now, been clearly separate matters: for example, natural and artistic beauty and makers and viewers of art. These are merely different instances of "sensibility." The domain that is thus constituted is what will be called the "aesthetic" domain.

The second move of Descartes's determination of the beautiful as the indeterminable consists in denying that the sensibility whose effect is beauty has any representational capacity. The sensory elements that together give rise to the impression of beauty, be it in the making or in the perception of a beautiful object, are without objective content.[4] Descartes says as much in his letter to Mersenne about judging something beautiful. Such a judgment does not vary according to the objects under consideration but according to the people who are considering the objects. The "aesthetic" judgment that an object is beautiful is not a judgment about the actual qualities of that object. Rather, it is the result of a variety of individual sensory impressions.

And what is true for the impression of beauty in the beholder's judgment is equally true for the impression of beauty in the art of painters, composers, and poets: they produce forms, but they do not represent forms. Neither the beholder's "aesthetic" taste nor a work of art's "aesthetic" merits have an objective quality that can be determined. Because they are instances of individual "sensibility," neither taste nor art can represent anything at all. If the first move in Descartes's theory of aesthetics consists in uniting various aspects of sensibility within the domain of the aesthetic, its second move consists in relieving this domain of any claim to representational capacity. A relief, a release, but to what end?

The content of sensible ideas consists of objects and their qualities. But according to Descartes, it is not essential that the qualities are "representations"—that is, representations of real objects and qualities. They *become* representations of reality only when my intellect "scrutinizes" and "examines" them (*Meditations*, III.19; 29⁵). At that point I can distinguish within them "the things which I perceive clearly and distinctly in them, [for example, their] . . . size, or extension in length, breadth and depth; [their] shape, which is a function of the boundaries of this extension; [their] position," and so on. By virtue of rational scrutiny of the objective elements of these objects—and not because of the sensory impressions they impart*—I know what they are:

> But as for all the rest, including light and colors, sounds, smells, tastes, heat and cold and the other tactile qualities, I think of these only in a very confused and obscure way, to the extent that I do not even know whether they are true or false, that is, whether the ideas I have of them are ideas of real things or of non-things. (ibid., 30)

Everything within the sensible ideation that eludes my scrutiny or clarification illustrates what sensible ideation is, in and of itself. Sensible ideas are not representations of real objects "from" which they "come." They cannot by their own power "resemble" them (III.11; 27), for by coming from an object, by being elicited by it, they always already transcend it. They add something to the impression that is received by the organs of sense and then transported to the "'common' sense."† Only in this way is it rendered an idea. This genesis of the idea out of a passively received impression is effected by the faculty of imagination, or fantasy. Rational scrutiny takes up its products, separating what is clear and

---

* "First, insofar as our external organs are all parts of the body, sense-perception, strictly speaking, is merely passive [*per passionem*] . . . in the same way in which wax takes on [*recipit*] an impression from a seal" (*Rules*, XII.5; 40).

† "Secondly, when an external sense organ is stimulated by an object, the figure which it receives is conveyed at one and the same moment to another part of the body known as the 'common' sense" (*Rules*, XII.7; 41).

distinct from what is obscure and confused, in order to transform an idea into a representation, a cognition, or a perception. Perception, according to Descartes, "is a case not of vision or touch or imagination . . . but of purely mental scrutiny" (*Meditations*, II.12; 21).

What is new here is not only the radicalization of the traditional reservation regarding the reliability of the senses, which becomes an attitude of fundamental doubt about their cognitive competence. What is new, first and foremost, is Descartes's justification for his claim that the intellect, by contrast, is just as fundamentally cognitively competent and capable of representing reality as the senses. This is because only the intellect—and not the senses—is capable of action. It is only for and by the intellect, then, that the Cartesian program "to reform my own thoughts and construct them upon a foundation which is all my own" (*Discourse*, II.3; 118)—a program in which epistemology and ethics intersect—can be enacted. Thoughts can be reformed, for to reform them means to construct them, setting out from "evident intuitions" and methodically constructing one upon the other in a regulated series of steps. Thoughts can be reformed because and to the extent that they are the "actions of the intellect" (*Rules*, III.4; 14); because and to the extent that we are capable of engendering them "by [our] own efforts [*propria industria*]" (*Rules*, X.I; 35) and by "guiding" and "curbing" ourselves in this process (*Discourse*, II.4; 119; *Meditations*, II.10; 20). The "foundation, which is all my own" and upon which Descartes wishes to "construct" his thoughts, is not one I *find* within myself. Rather, my foundation *is* myself. By making myself an agent and my thoughts my actions, I make myself the foundation upon which I can construct a performance that I enact and control step by step. Yet I can do this only in the domain of the intellect. Alternatively, the intellect is the only domain in which I can do this (*I* can *do* this), the only domain in which I am an "I." Descartes's belief that only the intellect is capable of cognition is grounded in his equation of cognitive competence with the capacity for action. It is with this equation—and *not* with the primacy of self-consciousness—that he initiates the modern concept of the subject.

In the domain of "sensibility," by contrast, there can be no "method" of progression because there cannot, in fact, be any sort of self-guided progression "which is all my own"—*hence* no cognition is possible. Just as Descartes grounds the cognitive capability of the intellect in its ability to act and, hence, to be "all my own [*tout à moi*]," he argues that the senses have no cognitive capacity because the process of sensibility is egoless and thus not an action. The antithesis of sensibility and intellect in Descartes has been described by this formulation: "If the vision of the eye is passive, that of the mind is active."[6] However, this antithesis of passivity and activity is, strictly speaking, misleading. Descartes speaks of passivity only occasionally and even then only with respect to the first step of sensibility—that which takes place in the sensory organs. The concept of activity, on the other hand, is also left relatively undefined as a distinguishing mark of the self-guided and self-controlled actions of the intellect. This double conceptual inadequacy—of linking the concept of passivity with sensibility and the concept of activity with the intellect—are both rooted in the operation of the imagination. The imagination belongs to the domain of sensibility, for it is incapable of endowing its ideas with any representational capacity or its images with any cognitive capacity. At the same time it is not just purely receptive, the mere imprint of an impression.* Unlike the common sense, it does not merely pass something on but, rather, produces and, indeed, *begins* something—something that is "quite different" from the impressions imprinted on it from outside. In other words, the imagination is generative and productive.

The concept of activity, then, requires further qualification if it is to account for the difference between the intellect and the imagination. *Both* are agencies that produce something—domains of "activity." Descartes's efforts to come to a new understanding of the interrelation of intellect and sensibility, which is required to make cognition possible, thus concerns not the interrelation of passivity and activity, of receptivity

---

* The "common" sense is the mechanism of an immediate impact, in "exactly the same way . . . that while I am writing, at the very moment when individual letters are traced on the paper, not only does the point of the pen move, but the slightest motion of this part cannot but be transmitted simultaneously to the whole pen" (*Rules*, XII.7; 41). The imagination or *phantasia*, by contrast, "can be the cause of many different movements in the nerves, even though it does not have images of these movements imprinted on it but has certain *other* images which enable these movements to follow on. Again, the pen as a whole does not move in exactly the same way as its lower end; on the contrary, the upper part of the pen seems to have a *quite different* and opposite movement" (ibid., XII.9; 42).

and spontaneity, of receiving and producing; it concerns the interrelation of two modes of performance of what he calls *ingenium*. What distinguishes them becomes clear as Descartes asks how the imagination can "hinder" the intellect, which "alone . . . is capable of knowledge," "so that we may be on our guard, and in what respect [the imagination can be] an asset, so that we may make full use of [its] resources" (*Rules*, VIII.9; 32). The intellect requires the resources of the imagination, for example, when a physical object comes under consideration, the idea of which "must be formed as distinctly as possible in the imagination" (XII.11; 43). Yet for this to happen, the imagination must be brought under the guidance of the intellect; the intellect must have command over the imagination. Now, this does not mean that the self-governance of the imagination is supplanted by an external "command" or governance exercised by the intellect, for the truth is that the imagination has no self-governance. *All* governance is external and foreign to it. All governance of the intellect is, by contrast, self-governance. That is the difference between the modes in which the imagination and the intellect perform and produce. The imagination is anarchic and undisciplined, and that is why it not only must be—but also can be—subject to the guidance of the intellect in its methodical progression. But why is external regulation necessary? On its own, the imagination is aimless and unpredictable; it does not pursue its own direction; thus it can be directed at will.[7]

PATHOLOGICAL EFFECTS

Descartes considers, with a certain degree of equanimity, the play of sensible impressions that expresses various aspects of the indeterminacy of the beautiful, fully aware of their powers to help and even to heal. In a letter to Princess Elizabeth, he recommends that, in order to steel herself against melancholy and to preserve her spiritual well-being, she "be like people who convince themselves they are thinking of nothing because they are observing the greenness of a wood, the colors of a flower, the flight of a bird, or something else requiring no attention."[8] This is the precise opposite of the effect that the insight into the capriciousness of the senses has on Pascal. In the *Pensées*, Descartes's doubt rises to the level of despair:

He who will know fully the vanity of man has only to consider the causes and effects of love. The cause is a *je ne sais quoi* (Corneille*), and the effects are dreadful. This *je ne sais quoi*, so small an object that we cannot recognize it, agitates a whole country, princes, armies, the entire world.

Cleopatra's nose: had it been shorter, the whole aspect of the world would have been altered.[9]

Because the beautiful image perceived by the senses is of indeterminable origin and content, Descartes considers dismissing it as merely an amusing play or diversion. For Pascal, however, it is precisely *because* the sensible image of the beautiful is indeterminable that it is endowed with a profoundly alarming power that agitates "the entire world."

In the appendix following the first part of his *Ethics* ("Of God"), Spinoza interpreted this power of sensible images as the effect of a process of metonymic inversion, the primal model of ideology: "it regards as an effect that which is in fact a cause, and vice versa."[10] Terms such as:

Good, Bad, Order, Confusion, Hot, Cold, Beauty, Ugliness . . . Praise, Blame, Right, Wrong . . . are nothing but modes of imagining whereby the imagination is affected in various ways, and yet the ignorant consider them as important attributes of things because they believe—as I have said—that all things were made on their behalf, and they call a thing's nature good or bad, healthy or rotten and corrupt, according to its effect on them. For instance, if the motion communicated to our nervous system by objects presented through our eyes is conducive to our feeling of well being, the objects which are its cause are said to be beautiful, while the objects which provoke a contrary motion are called ugly. . . . All this goes to show that everyone's judgment is a function of the disposition of his brain, or rather, that he mistakes for reality the way his imagination is affected. (241–42)

The error committed here is one of judgment: the sensible images that cause "the imagination" to be "affected in various ways" are erroneously taken to be qualities of the things themselves. It is an error judgment

---

* "Souvent je ne sais quoi qu'on ne peut exprimer / Nous surprend, nous emporte et nous force d'aimer" (Pierre Corneille, *Médée*, II.5; C.M.).

commits because it does not let itself be guided by the intellect (*Medita-tions*, IV.8; 103–5). It is an error judgment commits because the intellect is perhaps still weak and unpracticed—and perhaps also because it is momentarily "taking a holiday" (*Rules*, X.5; 36). In any case, it is an error judgment commits due to a false impression provoked by the imagination. This illustrates the power of the imagination: it has the ability to take the intellect's place in making a judgment.

What is needed, then, at least for the purposes of the critique of ideology—for the latter is rooted in the argument against the inversions of sensible judgment—is a more complex concept of the imagination. Such a concept must not only acknowledge that the imagination produces its images capriciously but also tell us why these images cannot be representations, that is, why imagination cannot constitute cognition. Moreover, it must also explain why its images are so able to impress us that we cannot scrutinize them with the intellect and—to Pascal's lasting alarm—simply judge them for what they are. Even describing the "dreadful" consequences of imagination gone awry requires an entirely different way of understanding the imagination. This new set of concepts must be able to do justice to the "formative power ('force') of the imaginative 'impressions.'"[11] Nonetheless, it must also explain how it gives these impressions such power, insistence, and clarity. Descartes's contrast between the different modes in which imagination and intellect operate can explain only why sensory images have no grounding in reality or reason. Still, his discussion of the lack of rules governing the imagination, of its haphazardness and arbitrariness, cannot explain why it is able to wield such great power.

THE "INTERNAL PRINCIPLE" OF THE SENSIBLE

Descartes's discussion of the beautiful performs two moves that are of foundational significance for the program of a philosophical aesthetics. The first consists in defining the aesthetic domain as the sphere of the "sensible." This permits a fusion of previously distinct elements—such as the theories of the arts (poetics) and of the beautiful (metaphysics)—in one and the same domain. The second move consists in describing the sensible as being without solid grounding or reason (*raison*) and, hence, of irreducible indeterminacy (*ce qui ne saurait être déterminé*). For within this sensible world operates the imagination—ungoverned by any rule. We can enjoy the pleasurable ideas and fantasies its unbounded freedom provides, or we can subject it to the control of its the opposite—the self-guided intellect—and use it as an auxiliary cognitive resource.

With these two moves, Descartes breaks with the traditions of both the poetic-rhetorical rules of art and the metaphysical theories of beauty. (The idea of an artistic classicism that might reconstruct these traditions on a Cartesian basis is paradoxical.[12]) At the same time, he destroys once and for all the possibility of defining—on the basis of their objective, representational content—either the beautiful or the arts. In this respect, his double move is foundational for the program of a philosophical aesthetics. In fact, it makes such a program possible in the first place. But this program does not limit itself to retracing Descartes's moves. Rather, it begins with the attempt to answer the question Descartes left unanswered, the question he had been the first to ask: how to conceive of the indeterminacy of the beautiful, as an effect of the imagination, in view of its overwhelming power. For the latter remains not understandable as long as the activity of the imagination is conceived merely as anarchic, even random.

The first philosopher to express the major contribution that will answer this question—and provide the fundamental concept that will set and keep aesthetics in motion—is Leibniz.[13] His decisive contribution is the idea that, just as the self-conscious and self-guided "actions of the intellect" have an "internal principle," so, too, do the sensible ideas. "Perceptions"—and these are, first and foremost, unconscious perceptions—constitute the "natural changes" of the monads, which "proceed from an *internal principle*.* For an external cause cannot influence their inner makeup."†[14] The "natural changes" of the monad consist in its producing ever-new perceptions, which are neither the effect of an external cause nor some sort of chaotic discharge. Rather, they reflect changes in the monad's own immanent impulses:

---

* Leibniz's draft adds: "that one can call an active force."
† Leibniz's draft adds a §12, which he later discarded: "And one can say, generally, that Force is nothing but the principle of change."

> The action of the internal principle which brings about the change or the passage from one perception to another may be called *appetition*. It is true that appetite cannot always attain altogether the whole perception to which it tends, but it always obtains some part of it, and so attains new perceptions. (*Monadology*, §15; 79)

That this process is the expression of an internal principle is sufficient to render it an activity. The awareness of what we are doing at any moment is not a necessary condition for our doing to be an activity. There is also a doing of which we are "unconscious," even a doing in a "daze" (*étourdissement**). Leibniz, unlike Descartes, can call even the genesis of sensible ideas an "*internal* [*action*]" of the soul (§17; 83) because he completely rethinks the idea of "internal principle." Rather than limiting it to the intellectual capacity of the I, which, by scrutinizing itself, has made itself its own foundation and can now methodically guide itself, he extends it to include unconscious "impulses" und "forces."[15] According to Leibniz's radical reconception, the genesis of any sensible idea is a movement of transition from a previous to a new "perception"—a movement of transition that is not haphazard and without rule but guided by an inner impulse:

> [E]very perception leads to a new perception, just as every movement that it represents leads to another movement. But it is impossible that the soul can know clearly its whole nature, and perceive how this innumerable number of small perceptions, piled up or rather concentrated together, shapes itself there: to that end it must needs know completely the whole universe which is embraced by them, that is, it must needs be a God.[16]

With these words, Leibniz writes the program of philosophical aesthetics. It calls for a way of understanding sensible ideas, which are by their very nature indeterminate, as the products neither of an unruly and chaotic imagination nor of self-conscious and self-guided actions on the part of the I. Rather, Leibniz sees them as the expression of a movement guided by a "principle" that is no less "internal" for being unconscious.

---

* Rendered in *Monadology* as "unconsciousness" (§§23, 24; 98, 101).

Aesthetics is a different way of *conceiving* sensibility. It is not merely a reevaluation of sensibility, although it is that, too, because it involves a redescription of sensibility. Aesthetics is a way of thinking that conceives the indissoluble indeterminacy of sensibility in conjunction with its internally guided, principled activity. The sensible is radically indeterminate because its generation of ideas cannot be reduced to self-conscious and self-controlled acts, performances of methodical operations of the intellect. At the same time, the ideas generated by the senses are neither a mere confluence of causal effects nor a haphazard and arbitrary play but an internal, though unconscious, operation belonging to the imagination. (This explains why Pascal found the power of sensible ideas so alarming: they do not derive from a reason that is amenable to the intellect.) The program of aesthetics aims to think about sensibility as a phenomenon beyond the Cartesian alternatives of self-conscious actions and causal mechanism, of self-guidance and haphazard projection. Indeed, it must reconsider these very alternatives and reconceptualize our ideas of knowledge and action, of play and imagination.

FORCE AND FACULTY

Leibniz's anti-Cartesian call for a mode of thinking that conceives of the imagination of sensible ideas as an activity propelled by an internal principle is the program of aesthetics. Aesthetics is the attempt to consider the internal principle of sensibility and, hence, to think of sensibility as an activity *without* retracting Descartes's definition of the sensible as the indeterminable. However, pervading even the words Leibniz himself finds for this "aesthetic" desideratum is an inner tension that will unfold, in the attempts to elaborate an aesthetic theory undertaken in immediate response to Leibniz, into an interminable and irreconcilable contention that continues to this day. "At every moment," Leibniz writes, "there is in us an infinity of perceptions, unaccompanied by awareness or reflection."[17] "They constitute that *je ne sais quoi*, those flavors," in which Leibniz distinguishes two aspects, now emphasizing one, now the other. The first aspect is that these perceptions enable us—in a way that according to Descartes's theory sensibility is incapable of doing—to grasp the things around us adequately, although not consciously and methodically. The second aspect is that there is an efficacy or power to these perceptions that far exceeds that exercised by the judgments of the intellect, a power that draws us into an infinite "sequence" of images engendered by and transforming into one another that confounds the intellect. In the first aspect, the "internal principle" of sensible activity presents itself as a *faculty*: the faculty of engendering sensible cognitions that are as indeterminable as they are adequate. (This will be Baumgarten's definition of the object and the program of his aesthetics.) In the second aspect, the "internal principle" of sensible activity presents itself as a *force*: the force propelling an ongoing transformation of the unconscious ideas that constitute us. (This will be how Herder, in a critique of Baumgarten, will refound aesthetics.) The issue of whether the internal principle of the movement in which sensible ideas are engendered must be thought of as a faculty of cognitive practices or as a force of unconscious expression is a contention that has riven the domain of aesthetics since its invention.[18] Moreover, it is, at the same time, a contention over how we must think of the human being.

CHAPTER TWO

Praxis: The Practice of the Subject

JE NE SAIS QUOI—"I know not what"—was the answer rationalist philosophy gave to the question of what is going on in the domain of the senses. The subject, imagining ideas of a sensory nature, knows not what these are, and philosophy cannot know where such ideation comes from—only that it proceeds capriciously and without rule. The sensible imagination is radically indeterminate: it does not arrive at determinations, and it eludes philosophical determination. However, once the domain of the senses is conceived as an "action" in accordance with an "internal principle," it can indeed be examined. This was the step Leibniz took, which opened up the field of "aesthetic inquiry." "Aesthetics," according to Baumgarten's first usage of the word in his dissertation on poetry,[1] means "philosophical inquiry into the *aisthētá*."* Thus, ipso facto, the aesthetic can be subjected to philosophical inquiry. Baumgarten's decisive step, which earned him the title of the "inventor"[2] of aesthetics, consists in understanding that an idea that comes from the senses is an object of philosophical inquiry *just like* an idea derived from the intellect. To inquire philosophically into the latter means to find out how the intellect must proceed in order to be successful in normative terms and attain the good for which it exists—the representation of the world. The fundamental move of aesthetics in the sense Baumgarten gave to it consists in showing that the sensible, too, *can* be subjected to a philosophical inquiry of this sort.

---

*"The Greek philosophers and the Church fathers have always carefully distinguished between αἰσθητά and νοητά . . . .So let the νοητά, what is known by the superior faculty, be the object of logic, and the αἰσθητά, the object of the ἐπιστήμη αἰσθητική or *aesthetics*" (*Poetry*, §CXVI; translation modified).

SENSIBLE CLARITY

In a short essay titled "Meditations on Knowledge, Truth, and Ideas," Leibniz expressed the thought that would form the basis of Baumgarten's conception of an "aesthetics." Leibniz writes that sensible ideas—that is to say, ideas we form via the senses, for example, ideas of "colors, odors, flavors," and the like—can likewise be "clear," as opposed to "obscure," when they make "it possible for me to recognize the thing represented."[3] My idea of the color red or my idea of a face is clear if and only if I can recognize the color or the face on the basis of previous sensory evidence:

> Thus we know colors, odors, flavors, and other particular objects of the senses clearly enough and discern them from each other but only by the simple evidence of the senses and not by marks that can be expressed. So we cannot explain to the blind man what red is, nor can we explain such a quality to others except by bringing them into the presence of the thing and making them see, smell, or taste it, or at least by reminding them of some similar perception they have had in the past. Yet it is certain that the concepts of these qualities are composite and can be resolved, for they certainly have their causes [*causas suas*].[4]

My knowledge of what red is does not require that my idea of this color be "distinct" or that it be expressed in the form of a definition. Nonetheless, I can give the reasons that I call it red (by indicating, for instance, the other objects I call "red"), and these reasons are intelligible to those who are already familiar with colors. This familiarity is the basis of sensible cognition. Sensible ideas, then, are distinguished by being indefinable. A "distinct concept," by contrast, is one "of which we have a *nominal definition*, which is nothing but the enumeration of sufficient marks."[5]

Sensible ideas, Leibniz writes, are "at once clear and confused" and not "obscure" (*New Essays*, 255). Leibniz thus splits the *je ne sais quoi*—by means of which Descartes had defined the domain of the senses as indeterminate and, thus, indeterminable—into two aspects. Because I know that my ideas of sensible realities, such as colors or faces, come only "through examples," I must, "until their inner structure has been deciphered . . . say that they are a *je ne sais quoi*" (ibid.). At the same time, however, my ideas of these sensory realities are sufficient because I "recognize [these colors and faces] and [can] easily tell them from one another" (ibid.). In other words, I know something even though I do not know it with the precision of a definition. By distinguishing between the ability to know and the ability to define, Leibniz transforms the domain of the senses into an object that is open to epistemological inquiry: the object of "aesthetics."

A restatement of Leibniz's move appears early in Baumgarten's reflections on poetry, which closes with the introduction of the term "aesthetics" (*Poetry*, §CXVI; see footnote on p. 13). Here Baumgarten rephrases Leibniz's distinction between "obscure" and "clear" as follows:

> In obscure representations there are not contained as many representations of characteristic traits as would suffice for recognizing them and for distinguishing them from others and as, in fact, are contained in clear representations (by definition). (*Poetry*, §XIII; 41)

Baumgarten goes on to state that the clarity of ideas is independent of their distinctness and their ability to be defined. Sensible ideas, too, can be clear, and they are clear when they enable us to recognize a thing or a quality—to recognize something *as* something. Sensible cognition, according to Baumgarten, is "the totality of those representations which remain beneath distinctness." Sensible cognition—and only on the basis of this argument can it be called "cognition"—shares this feature with intellectual cognition. Nonetheless, sensible cognition is *like* intellectual cognition—the "analog of reason."[6]

The structural analogy of sensibility and reason refers to the idea that sensible cognition, as *re*cognition, must be conceived of as an ongoing, self-regulating process. Thus, every time I recognize an individual color or see a particular tree, I follow the same general principle of identifying what the idea of the specific color or tree consists in. Each individual act of sensible cognition, then, is structured in such a way that it must be conceived as the realization of a principle, as the application of something general. True, Baumgarten occasionally seems to say that definition is the ideal realization of the "principle" of cognition, that is, the ideal instance of generality, which makes recognition possible. However, with the insight that cognition in general "necessarily has an admixture of confusion," what becomes central is the structure that rational and sensible cognition evince in equal but different ways. Just as rational cognition is based on definition and sensible cognition is based on recognition, so both forms of cognition identify a particular object as the same as another and, hence, as another case of one and the same general principle. To the extent that sensible ideas exhibit this movement of the generation and application of a general principle, they, too, thus possess what Leibniz had called an "internal principle."

The most striking consequence of this new "aesthetic" perspective on sensibility is the fact that sensual ideation is no longer seen as a domain that is subject to the intellect, which can (and must) pass judgment on it from the outside. Instead, sensibility is considered as capable as rational cognition of making a normative judgment on its own terms; the distinction between right and wrong is internal to the sensible: "Thus there exists a good and a bad taste," a "perfect taste," which comprehends the perfections of an object, whereas someone "wanting in taste" can fail to grasp them.[7] Sensible observation and judgment grasp their object all of a sudden, "before all discussion." "Our intuitive sense tells us its nature, before we ever thought of inquiring into it."[8] To grasp the object as it is, is not a success that is external to the sensible ideas, a success that is ascertained and ensured by a scrutinizing intellect; it is the normative success that sensible ideation itself aims at and is capable of. From an aesthetic perspective, sensual ideation is capable of truth by virtue of its own power and without guidance from, or scrutiny by, the intellect.[9]

PRACTICING

Leibniz's "Meditations on Knowledge, Truth, and Ideas" can be said to contain the seed of an aesthetic theory subsequently elaborated by Baumgarten with respect to not only what he says about sensible ideation but also *how* he arrives at this insight, specifically, the form of evidence he claims for his reconception of the sensible. Immediately after noting that we have reasons—in the form of examples rather than definitions—for our sensible cognitions, Leibniz writes:

> Likewise we sometimes see painters and other artists correctly [*probe*] judge what has been done well or done badly; yet they are often unable to give a reason for their judgment but tell the inquirer that the

work which displeases them lacks "something, I know not what [ne-scio quid]." (291)

The praxis of artists becomes important to Leibniz at this point because it illustrates the idea that sensible perceptions and judgments can be called "correct" without being clear and distinct and, thus, without our defining the criteria by which the perceptions and judgments are being made. Artists and their praxis thus exemplify for Leibniz the ability—specific to sensibility—to perceive and judge without definite knowledge and, nonetheless, to achieve correct results. That is to say, it is an aesthetic reflection *in nuce*, a reflection on the praxis of the arts and artists, which leads Leibniz to the insight (or at least provides a new kind of evidence for it) that is fundamentally different from Descartes's: the sensible is a performance that can succeed or fail and, hence, is normative in itself. A regard for the arts in particular shifts Leibniz's understanding of sensibility, in general.

This shift reaches much further and is both more fundamental and more ambiguous than is indicated by the widespread formula that aesthetics is about a "positive reevaluation" or "rehabilitation" of the sensible. We have already seen that sensible ideation can be understood, *pace* Descartes, as a (another) form of clear cognition only if it is defined, again *pace* Descartes, as a (another) form of activity: to conceive of sensible ideation as a form of clear cognition means to understand it as a performance propelled by an "internal principle" and, hence (in accordance with Leibniz's use of the term; see p. 9), as an activity. However, aesthetics can succeed in this reconceptualization of the sensible as a mode of activity only if it revises the central concepts of modern philosophy, including and especially the Cartesian "I." Aesthetics achieves this additional foundational step by taking the experience of the arts—of creating them and thinking about them—seriously.

Baumgarten's aesthetics here focuses on an aspect that had already been emphasized by the contemporary theorists of taste. Sensible cognition, Abbé Dubos writes, rests on a natural disposition "improved [*perfectionné*] . . . by frequent use and experience."[10] Indeed, to have "confidence . . . in sense and practice" instead of clinging to the methodic procedures of the philosophers, who "[lay] down general principles, and . . . [draw] from thence a chain of conclusions," is, according to

Dubos, even a sign of maturity, of the perfection of human reason.[11] Hume, directly borrowing Dubos's terminology, writes similarly that we can attain "delicacy of taste" only by means of "practice."[12] As always, Baumgarten is the one who gives the most exhaustive (and exhausting) treatment of the subject of practice. Early in his *Aesthetics*, having redefined the sensible "by analogy," he examines the *"character of the successful aesthetician [felicis aesthetici]"* (*Aesthetics*, §27). The development of the latter requires not only, first, *"connate natural aesthetics . . . ,* the natural disposition of the entire soul for beautiful cognition, with which one is born," (§28) but also, second, "ἄσκησις [training] and *aesthetic exercise"* (§47):

> The nature [discussed in the preceding section] cannot remain on the same level even for a short time. . . . Hence it will decrease somewhat, however large one may posit it, unless its dispositions or its acquired character are fostered by ongoing exercises, and grow numb. (§48)

Practice, habit, and frequent use—aesthetics learns with regard to the arts—are the ways, indeed the *only* ways, to perfect the performances of sensibility. Practice, habit, and frequent use, then, are the aesthetic alternatives to the principle that had framed the rationalist project of reform: of either sensibility receiving external guidance from reason or reason progressing methodically within itself. The right practice is the right way to exercise "sovereign command, not despotic rule [*imperium . . . non tyrannis*]" (§12) over the sensory world: by power of sensibility itself, as aesthetically educated sensibility.

The attention to artistic practice offers aesthetics an insight not merely into the only adequate way of perfecting sensible performances but also into the "tyranny"—that is, the illegitimacy and, hence, inefficiency—of the program of guidance propagated by rationalism. That sensible performances can be perfected only through practice, habit, and frequent use also suggests the difference between rationality and the specific way in which the sensible must be conceived as a performance propelled by an "internal principle" and, hence, as "activity." I can practice only what I can do myself. That, after all, is the aim of practice: to be able to do it myself. And I *need not* practice what is at my arbitrary command. That, after all, is what makes practice necessary. Wanting to do something is not the same as being able to do it—let alone being able to do it well.

The insight into the importance of practice gained from the aesthetic attention to the arts provides a new insight into the nature of what is practiced—into the performative character of sensible perception and judgment. Sensible perception is my activity and not a mere passive impression or arbitrary effect. But I do not perform this activity as if I were abiding by a "method." I can abide by a method only where an activity—according to Descartes, the activity of the intellect—can be understood as the application of a previous knowledge of this activity that is independent of the performance of this activity. In other words, the activity is the application of a theory. That is what Descartes means by "reform[ing] my own thoughts and construct[ing] them upon a foundation which is all my own."[13] Practice shows that sensible perception can be an activity as well, but it is not an activity like *this*. It is not an activity that can be understood as the application of a theory about which the agent has a prior knowledge. The performance of the activity of sensibility is propelled by an internal principle that precedes and guides it but that cannot be detached from it and presented in the form of a theory.

THE SOUL IS SUBJECT

The answer to the question, how I am active in my sensible performances without being active in the sense of following a method or applying a theory, is this: I am "a specific subject" in the performances. This is Baumgarten's formulation in the chapter in his *Metaphysics* about the "inferior cognitive faculties," in which he resumes his definition of the concept of "aesthetics." Baumgarten introduces "into the technical language of philosophy the concept of 'subjectiveness' in the sense in which it has been current since Kant"[14] in order to draw conclusions from the program of an aesthetic examination of the sensible for philosophical "psychology."

> Easy is the realization that requires little force [*vis*]. The realization that requires greater force is difficult. Thus it is easy for a subject when realization demands only a small part of the force that makes him strong, and it is difficult when the realization requires a large part of the force that he possesses. (*Metaphysics*, §527)

In the traditional grammatical sense established by Boethius's translation of Aristotle's terminology, "subject" has meant a carrier of qualities
or predicates.[15] In Baumgarten, by contrast, "subject" becomes the name
of that "substance" which has "forces" (greater or smaller), whose "realization" (easier or more difficult) enables him to do something. Having
forces makes something or someone a "subject." It is in precisely this
sense that sensible performances are the activities of a subject because
we have to conceive of these performances in such a way that, in them,
the forces of a subject are realized. This should not be misconstrued to
imply psychological causality; the force a subject has is not some kind of
"cause" that brings about a particular event or activity. Rather, a subject's force explains the meaning of the "internal principle" of the activity.
Moreover, it was precisely the "internal principle" of the activity of sensible ideation that Leibniz had noted as a desideratum. How Baumgarten's
concept of the subject as an agency exercising forces relates to this "internal principle" is illustrated most clearly once again by the aesthetic
phenomenon of practice.

Practice aims at the acquisition of capabilities and proficiencies.
Through practice, we gain ability. To practice means to practice a praxis
so that we can then exercise it. What we gain in practice is a double ability: the ability to perform [ausführen] something and the ability to guide
[führen] ourselves. To have an ability means, first, to be able to perform
an activity successfully in accordance with its particular criteria of success. Thus to have an ability always means to be able to do something
good, to be able to realize the good of an activity. All performative ability requires, second, the ability to guide oneself, that is, to direct the
movements of one's own body and mind and correct their deviations in
accordance with the criteria of this activity. When the concept of the
subject is introduced, as it is by Baumgarten, on the basis of the praxis
of practice, then subjectivity is, fundamentally, the practical self-relation
of self-guidance that has its place, meaning, and criteria in the performance of something. To be a subject and to have an ability (in this
double sense of ability) are one and the same thing. To put it another
way: subjectivity is power or, more precisely, the power or ability to act.
To be a subject means to have power in a double sense: to be able to realize the good of an activity and be able to guide one's own movements
accordingly.

This means that aesthetics conceives of the subject as essentially practical. It is foundational for the subject that he can do something—that he has a capability or power: "My soul is force" (*Metaphysics*, §505). Aesthetically conceived, the subject is someone who is able. Only because and to the extent that he is able to do something is the subject also able to know and will something. The primary self-relation is not one of knowing but of self-guidance in active performance: subjectivity is the self-relation of and with forces. "Ability (or power) comes before knowledge" is the first insight that can be derived from the importance of practice for the concept of the subject. This immediately entails a second insight into the primacy of ability not only over knowledge but also over the will: I can will only what I am able to do—what I can perform and in what way I have the power or the faculty to guide myself. ("Action" is not a movement caused by my own intentions but a movement in which my own forces realize themselves.) Ability or power not only comes before knowledge; ability or power also comes before freedom.

This lends precise conceptual contours to the term "force" (*vis*), which Baumgarten uses interchangeably with "faculty" (*facultas*) and "proficiency" (*habitus*) to describe ability: in Baumgarten, "force" and "proficiency" both designate the *faculty of the subject*. And to have a faculty means to have the faculty to *do something*: to be able to perform, to realize something. This implies that a faculty is defined by what it can bring about. Its structure, then, is essentially teleological: it is related to a good or a sort of goodness. The relation between the faculty and the exercise of the faculty is not extrinsic and accidental (in the fashion of a moving object, which imparts the force that propels it toward everything it accidentally collides with) but internal and meaningful. To exercise a faculty *means* to realize the good toward which the particular faculty is directed. Failure to realize this good implies that the faculty has not been exercised—or that it has been exercised only inadequately or insufficiently. To have a faculty does not mean to generally cause some kind of effect but, rather, to be able to realize this particular good. To have a faculty means to be able to achieve the success of something.

That faculties are not defined (causally) by their effects but (teleologically) by their achievements also indicates their essential generality. *What* we are able to do is perform not merely an action but an activity or a *mode* of action. Of course, a subject always performs an individual act under a particular condition. Yet when we conceive of this act as the exercise of a faculty on the subject's part, we describe it not as a particular act but as a general activity. The subject's ability is always something general. I can *generally* be active in a certain mode, I can perform an activity in *general*—or not at all. For the same reason, however, what the subject is able to do is always particular. If I can be generally active in a certain mode, it implies that I can realize this general activity here and now, in this particular instance and in this particular fashion. If "force" must be understood, in Baumgarten's terms, as a subjective faculty, then the self-realization of a force consists in the particular realization of a general activity. And if we can call a general activity a "praxis," then the faculty of the subject consists in that subject's realization of, or participation in, a praxis.

On the basis of these considerations, we can define the aesthetic concepts of subjectivity and of sensibility as follows:

Subjectivity. If the realization of a force conceived as a faculty is the particular realization of a general activity, then the force is a general activity that has become internal and proper to the subject. The aesthetic conception of the subject defines the latter not as an agency confronting, and certainly not as an agency preceding, a praxis. Instead, by defining the subject by his forces conceived as faculties, aesthetics defines the subject as the agency performing this praxis—the agency of the performance of a general activity. The praxis is the subject's "property"—not in the sense that it is an external relationship but because praxis is what is proper to the subject and without it the subject is nothing. The aesthetic subject is also not something "internal" confronting the externality of general activities or practices. In fact, Baumgarten's aesthetic subject is, in his faculties, the reality of the general activity because he is the agency of his realization. Subjectivity consists in the ability to realize a praxis. At the same time, the praxis exists only because a subject can realize it. The point of the concept of the subject, which aesthetics develops with regard to practice and designates with the concept of faculty, is that the subject *defines* praxis and praxis *defines* the subject.[16]

Sensibility. If sensible performances are actions by virtue of the fact that their "internal principle" consists in the faculty of the subject, and if every realization of a force conceived as faculty is always the particular realization of a general activity, then the sensible, too, must be capable of being understood as such a general activity realized in individual sensible performances in circumstances that are, in each instance, particular. This is the basis on which the elements of the aesthetic examination of sensibility rest: (1) the idea of sensible clarity, (2) the significance of practice, and (3) the concept of the subject. First, sensible ideas are *clear* when they are acts of recognition and, hence, of an ongoing sensible praxis of perception. Second, sensible perception can, and indeed must, be *practiced* because practice is the way in which faculties are acquired. Third, sensible performances are *subjective* performances because their internal principle consists in the forces, conceived as faculties, of a subject.

THE INDIVIDUAL AND DISCIPLINE

The subject, as a fundamental concept of aesthetics, is at the center of the debate over the genesis and significance of philosophical aesthetics—that is, the debate about how we must understand modernity, one of whose defining features is the fact that it developed aesthetics. In his lectures and notes on Nietzsche between the years 1936 and 1945,[17] Heidegger argued that aesthetic modernity and the rationalist modernity of Descartes are one and the same. Aesthetics (or so Heidegger claimed to detect in reading its thoroughly developed form in Nietzsche's philosophy) is an application and not a critique of—a complement and not an alternative to—the "metaphysics of the modern age" founded by Descartes. Moreover, according to Heidegger, one and the same metaphysical "fundamental position" (*Nietzsche*, IV, 136) extends from Cartesian rationalism via the aesthetic treatises of the eighteenth century to Nietzsche's concept of the will. Heidegger claims that this is illustrated by the concept of the subject in aesthetics. Just as "certitude of all Being and all truth" is grounded in modern metaphysics "in the self-consciousness of the individual ego: *ego cogito ergo sum*," "[m]editation on the beautiful in art now slips markedly, even exclusively, into the relation to man's state of feeling, *aísthēsis*" (*Nietzsche*, I, 83; translation modified). In aesthetics, the work of art "is posited as the 'object' for a 'subject'; definitive for aesthetic consideration is the subject-object relation" (ibid., 78). About the sensible acts it scrutinizes, aesthetics maintains exactly what rationalist philosophy had said about the "actions of the intellect": that "the *self* of man is essential as what lies at the very ground. The self is *sub-iectum*" (*Nietzsche*, IV, 108). The debate over the modern genesis and significance of philosophical aesthetics cannot grasp its essential impact until we abandon this circuitous interpretation of the aesthetic subject as metaphysical ground, as a mere repetition of the Cartesian I—because the aesthetic subject is the principle of its sensible performances only because it is a *participant* of a social praxis that it both enacts and represents.

In the debate over aesthetics that has erupted after and *beyond* Heidegger, both sides agree that their dispute concerns the meaning of the new aesthetic conception of the subject. Joachim Ritter, a paradigmatic representative of the interpretation that dominates the discussion in Germany, argues that the aesthetic subject is the "counterweight" balancing the rational subject formed by the objectified society of modernity.[18] Whereas the modern subject in society's economic, scientific, technological, administrative, and juridical institutions bears an objective and impersonal countenance, the human being realizes himself in the act of "aesthetic appresentation"—whose exemplary object is nature—as a "sentient" being that encounters a world full of life and meaning. The aesthetic subject forms "organs . . . that keep the richness of the human being present, something society could not realize or express without them" ("Landschaft," 163). In this context, Ritter emphasizes—against cultural revolutionaries on the left, as well as the right—that rational objectification and aesthetic vitality are inseparable, precisely because they run counter to one another:

> Schiller conceives aesthetic art as the organ that the spirit develops on the basis of society in order to restore to man, to recover for him, what society, in the reification of the world into its object, which is necessary for it, must externalize. The nature into which man's life on earth belongs, as heaven and earth, becomes aesthetic in the landscape, as the content of the freedom on whose existence society and its domination of an objectified and subjected nature is predicated. ("Landschaft," 162)

The aesthetic subject is part of the "personal being of the individual" that has been "severed" and "isolated" (*entzweit*) from his "social being"[19]—but only in modern society. The aesthetic is one side of the social division of the social.

Ritter emphasizes that the aesthetic subject is structurally different from the objective-rational subject in the way in which he relates to the object. He describes this aesthetic relation as the vivid appresentation of an object in the totality of its meaning. In doing so, he takes up a key feature of the aesthetic Baumgarten had already explicated, for the definition of the sensible as an indefinable ("confused"), clear cognition is merely the point of departure. The aim of aesthetic practice is to perfect the confused clarity of the sensible in such a way that it becomes capable of perceiving its object in the "richness" of its "singular" qualitative character (*Aesthetics*, §440), in its "aesthetic truth" (§423). It is precisely because the sensible is both clear *and* confused that it can do something that reason is incapable of,* namely, perceive the object as an "individual." Baumgarten calls the quality taken on by such aesthetic perception liveliness or vividness (*vividitas*):

> We call that vivid in which we are allowed to perceive many parts, either simultaneously or in succession. (*Poetry*, §CXII; 76)
>
> That is why I think I can rightly call only those thoughts vivid in which I apprehend a certain peculiar variety and a sudden celerity as though of features that press upon one another, out of the uncommonly wide diffusion of which may rise that luster and splendor of meditation which, in its entirety, must nonetheless be perspicuous and absolutely clear. (*Aesthetics* §619)

---

* "As the universal objects of human disciplines and sciences have in this fashion come into existence, thus also arises in the souls of well-educated people a perfect, often beautiful and, even in the stricter sense, logical truth. Yet at once the question is asked, whether metaphysical truth be adequate to such a universal as it is to the individual contained under it? I do indeed think that it can now be perfectly obvious to philosophers that cognition and logical truth could only, with a sacrifice of much and great material perfection, be made to acquire whatever there is in them of especial formal perfection. For what is abstraction if not a loss? By the same token, you would not be able to make out of a marble of irregular shape a marble globe without losing at least as much material as the greater value of roundness would exact" (*Aesthetics*, §560).

The vivid aesthetic idea has a diversity and variety that are determined by the law of similarity—thus leading to sensible clarity.[20] The corresponding quality on the side of the aesthetic subject is the "consensus" (*Aesthetics*, §47) of its faculties, a quality the aesthetic subject, *felix aestheticus*, has acquired in aesthetic practice. The aesthetic subject—based on Baumgarten's remarks in the context of Ritter's interpretation—can perceive the object in its sensible individuality beyond or before all general concepts only because, out of the impressions he produces *within himself*, he receives a vivid totality that is individual and not predetermined by any general rule. The aesthetic subject is the free and living individual, engendering the truth of his particular object out of himself.

That the aesthetic subject is new and fundamentally different from the rationalist I—this objection against Heidegger is also the point of departure for the opposite interpretation of aesthetics, offered by Michel Foucault. Foucault unfolds this interpretation indirectly, without mentioning aesthetics or the authors who contributed to it, in the manner in which he describes, in *Discipline and Punish*, the new type of power that developed in the century of the Enlightenment, displacing that defined by sovereignty.[21] Foucault's description of this new type of disciplinary power is replete with the terms of philosophical aesthetics, which emerged during the same era. The body on which this disciplinary power focuses its energy is no longer the mechanical body, "the image of which had for so long haunted those who dreamt of disciplinary perfection. This new object is the natural body, the bearer of forces and the seat of duration" (*Discipline*, 155). The individual is constituted as

> a describable, analyzable object, not in order to reduce him to "specific" features, as did the naturalists in relation to living beings, but in order to maintain him in his individual features, in his particular evolution, in his own aptitudes or abilities, under the gaze of a permanent corpus of knowledge. (190)

The central terms of Foucault's characterization of the body of disciplinary power are natural or organic individuality, force and ability, dynamics, development, and practice (156–62)—in other words, the terms of the emerging aesthetic philosophy. The discipline of aesthetics is the aesthetics of discipline.

This is also why aesthetics, following Foucault's objection against Cassirer,[22] cannot be understood in isolation, on the basis of "philosophy and reflection." What the metaphysics of the aesthetic subject is really about is something only the microphysics of disciplinary power can teach us: the aesthetic subject is both "an effect and an object" of disciplines. Disciplinary power controls the living bodies so as to develop their capabilities and "[bend their] behaviour toward a terminal state." Disciplinary power controls bodies by *exercising* them: "Exercise is that technique by which one imposes on the body tasks that are both repetitive and different, but always graduated" (*Discipline*, 161). Aesthetic practice, we read in Baumgarten, is a "frequent repetition of homogeneous actions such that a sort of consensus comes into being between the mind and the inborn character ... with respect to a given topic" (*Aesthetics*, §47). The "vivid" consensus of faculties and ideas is the result of a disciplinary practice Baumgarten compares to the exercises of soldiers (§49)—the very paradigm of discipline (cf. *Discipline*, 179–80). As it turns out, the success of such practice depends, to a large extent, on whether it has been correctly adjusted according to the level of development attained by the practicing subject. In practice, we learn "whether and to what extent the forces of a given man suffice for a given beautiful cognition" (*Aesthetics*, §61). Practice produces knowledge of the human being. It was "from such trifles"—the great variety of practice exercises, surveillances, examinations, and sanctions that constitute disciplinary power—that the subject, "the man of modern humanism," investigated by the human sciences, "was born" (*Discipline*, 141, and cf. 183). What becomes obvious in practice is that subjectivization is discipline—and discipline is subjectivization:

> At the heart of the procedures of discipline, it manifests the subjection [*assujettissement*: subjection and subjectivization, CM] of those who are perceived as objects and the objectification of those who are subjected. (184–85)

What is new about disciplinary power is that it is a subjection that turns those who are its objects into "subjects." If we read the new aesthetic theory of the subject according to Foucault, we see that it expresses a new type of social power: the aesthetic science of the subject as an agency exercising forces that call for practice. Aesthetics is not the "counterweight" (as Ritter would have it) against social discipline but simultaneously the instrument and ideology of social discipline.[23]

———————

THE AESTHETIC CONCEPT OF the subject contradicts the rationalist concept of the I by insisting on the insight that the subject can be the "internal principle" of actions only if he is a component of and a participant in social practices. This means that the good of social practices has no "objective" existence independent of the subject. Rather, the good of the practices exists only in the performances of the subject. Aesthetic philosophy is enlightenment: it enlightens us regarding the fact that the good of practices has its reality in the abilities, the faculties, of the subject—or else it has no reality at all. Aesthetic philosophy is enlightenment because its concept of the subject divests the good of its transcendent reality: aesthetics is enlightenment as a subjectivization of the good.

The debate over the interpretation of aesthetics is a debate over the interpretation of the enlightenment, specifically, the specific move of the enlightenment by which aesthetics leaves behind the rationalist dualism of body and mind, of sensibility and reason, and conceives of the subject such that *both* sensibility *and* reason are actions of the subject. Both are performances propelled by an internal principle, performances exercising subjective faculties. The debate over the interpretation of aesthetics is really about how to understand its subjectivization of the sensible—that is, its sensibilization of the subjective.

According to Ritter's interpretation, aesthetics demonstrates that the enlightenment process of subjectivization suffers from a profound alienation: between the objective-rational subject of social institutions and the personal-sentient subject of the aesthetic relation to the self and the world. Aesthetic subjectivization is an internal countermovement against the enlightenment's objectification of the world: the development of potentials of enlivening individualization. *According to Foucault's interpretation*, by contrast, aesthetics demonstrates that the enlightenment process of subjectivization succumbs to a tendency to totalize—a tendency to submit the sensible to precisely those processes of subjectivization that rationalistic thinking had reserved for the domain of the mind. It is precisely by comprising the sensible that the enlightenment subjectivization proves to be a program of normalizing discipline. These two interpretations mark the extremes between which the debate over the modern genesis and significance of aesthetics vacillates.

Yet whether the aesthetic subjectivization is interpreted as an individualization or as a program of discipline—whether aesthetics is conceived as a thinking of a "relieving" (Odo Marquard), even an "emancipation" (Herbert Marcuse), or of a "colonialization" (Terry Eagleton) of the sensible—both Ritter's and Foucault's readings presuppose that aesthetic thinking is a thinking of the subject and that aesthetics can be subsumed under enlightenment. Both the individual, who, as Ritter describes him, perceives in various ideas the individual truth of his object, and the disciplined participant, who, as Foucault describes him, is produced and reproduced by exercises practicing his forces—these two are both "subjects." Their soul is the seat of faculties for the realization of social practices. Ritter and Foucault merely emphasize one of the two sides of this single aesthetic conception of the subject: that subjective faculties, once they have been acquired, can be put to individual use and that subjective faculties must initially be produced in processes of discipline.

Yet the thinking of aesthetics contains a challenge more profound than the question of how to combine individualization and discipline, a challenge relating to the concept of the subject initially developed by aesthetics. Baumgarten was the first to identify this challenge—but he did not resolve it—when he concluded from its "confused" nature that something "obscure" operates in *all* sensibility. "He who thinks something confusedly," he wrote, "has obscure representations of something" (*Metaphysics*, §510). There is a "field of obscurity" (§514) in the soul that remains impervious to illumination, for paradoxically, its very obscurity is the precondition for the existence of clarity:

> There are in the soul obscure perceptions. Their totality is called the ground of the soul [*fundus animae*]. (§511)

What consequences must this insight that the "ground" of the soul is "obscure" have for the conviction that the soul is "subject"?

CHAPTER THREE

Play: The Operation of Force

CRITICS SINCE MEIER HAVE praised Baumgarten as the "inventor" of aesthetics, who elaborated into a comprehensive theory Leibniz's program of thinking unconscious sensibility as another "activity" propelled by an "internal principle." Baumgarten chooses the concept of "sensible cognition" as the point of departure for a systematic reconception of central elements from the dialectical, rhetorical, and poetical traditions. Aesthetics, he writes, is "the science of sensible cognition" and, as such, is a "theory of the liberal arts, science of the lower cognitive faculties, art of thinking beautifully, art of the analog of reason."* This elaboration of a unified theory is possible because Baumgarten decisively reframes the program Leibniz had formulated using the traditional Aristotelian terminology. Baumgarten explicates Leibniz's "internal principle" of sensible activity as a "faculty of the subject." He could "invent" aesthetics because he was able to secure sensibility's claim to the status of cognition by interpreting it as an activity of the subject.

For this same reason, however, Herder, in a series of sketches for a "monument" to Baumgarten that have remained incomplete drafts, regarded the latter's aesthetics as a dead end: "The author's errors enmesh . . . the entire book into a series of missteps that are much too closely interwoven with the entire edifice of his science."[1] Baumgarten, maintains Herder, is the inventor not of aesthetics as such but of an *"aesthetics after the Baumgartian manner"* ("Monument," 48). "An aesthetics

---

* *"Aesthetics* (theory of the liberal arts, science of the lower cognitive faculties, art of thinking beautifully, art of the analog of reason) is the science of sensible cognition" (*Aesthetics*, §1).

after the Greek manner" would be a better term, for only such a description reflects "what its name declares it to be: *aesthetics*, the science of feeling" (49). As such, it is "by far *wider [latior]*" and also "far *briefer* than and entirely *different* from" Baumgarten's ["Baumgarten," 665]). By treating the sensible, his point of departure, not as feeling but as cognition, Baumgarten obscured and concealed, rather than invented, aesthetics—or what aesthetics, rightly understood, ought to be. What Herder's critique of Baumgarten calls for ("Monument," 49–50) is a reconception of aesthetics as the thinking of an "internal principle" of sensible activity that is not—yet—a subjective faculty; a reconception of aesthetics as a thinking of force. "Now that would be aesthetics!"

AESTHETIC GENEALOGY

According to Herder's critique, the very first paragraph of Baumgarten's *Aesthetics* expresses a double confusion that is ultimately rooted in a single fundamental conceptual failure. The first confusion, Herder claims, concerns the relationship between "theory" and "art," between "philosophical scrutiny" and instruction or "proficiency" ("Baumgarten," 659). Baumgarten's aesthetics is meant to be both, but what is their relationship? The second confusion, Herder argues, distorts the definition of the object of aesthetics, that is, of "sensible cognition":

> Just as thinking is not the first thing in the human being . . . beautiful *cognition* is not the beginning of aesthetics. The human being, the animal, first *senses . . . obscurely;. . . .* then senses . . . vividly; and senses, obscurely, pleasure and pain within himself; then senses *pleasure and pain* clearly outside himself; and only now does he have *cognition.* In just this same fashion, [we] must examine the subjective order of the beautiful. But this grows out of the false philosophical root. The essence of the soul is the cognitive faculty; hence the first thing about the beautiful must be, it is a *thought:* When this proposition is presented plainly, it is false: *vide infra.* And if, in order to examine beauty, I begin with the beauty of thought, it is doubly false: for first I must encounter the former, the latter ought to come at the end. (670)

The fundamental error of Baumgarten's aesthetics consists in its confusion of the first with the last, of what comes before with what comes after. Its examination begins too late, on a level and with a class of operations and a type of faculty that emerge only later, that are not "the first." Baumgarten's aesthetics thus misinterprets these operations and this faculty as the "root," or "ground"—when, in fact, we understand them correctly only if we consider them as the result of an earlier foundation that is concealed within them.

What Herder says elsewhere about "taste" also holds true for Baumgarten's "sensible cognition." It is therefore "not a fundamental faculty, a universal fundamental faculty of the soul; it is a habitual application of our judgment to objects of beauty. Let us trace its genesis."[2] This is the program of an aesthetics that seeks to gain insight into the "genesis" of all manners of judgment and cognition, down to and including the sensible or confused cognition with which Baumgarten begins, out of the "most hidden ground of the soul." Only in this way, by scrutinizing the ground that precedes them—and not by examining them in isolation—can we gain a clear understanding of the modes of judgment and cognition, be they definitive and distinct or sensible and confused. "Since the most hidden ground of the soul harbors the most powerful springs that drive the more well-known ones," Baumgarten writes, "it would be in vain to labor to arrive, setting out from this intermediate object, at either end; here, then, let the aesthetician dig" ("Baumgarten," 671). Herder reconceives aesthetics as an archaeology or, more precisely, as a genealogy—an inquiry into origin and genesis.

The general methodological objection Herder raises against an "aesthetics after the Baumgartian manner" is that, instead of exploring man as the scene and process of the subject's formation, it persists in the old error of the "wise men of our world" (Cognition, 212). Its starting point is what something has become rather than its having become something, that is, its becoming. In order to know what man does and can do, one must explore how he became what he is. Herder also understands this methodological turn toward genealogy as a consequence of the program he had early on called a "contraction of philosophy to anthropology."[3] Man's knowledge of himself does not consist in knowing that he is a subject but in knowing how he has become a subject. Man's anthropological self-reflection—"O man! become acquainted with yourself" ("Baumgarten," 688)—pierces the illusory images created by a philosophy (and a culture) that begins too late, with a subject that has already become.

But why does this program of a genealogical self-reflection form the basis of the program of an *aesthetics*? Why can anthropology be realized only *as* aesthetics? The answer to these questions can be found in Herder's identification of the "aesthetics *after the Greek manner*" as a "science of feeling." The exploration of man as he is before he becomes a subject is a regression to the "beginning," as a regression to the "ground." "This is a piece of the *most necessary* anthropology, for our *strength* as *human beings* consists in the *ground* of our souls" (665).

Another term Herder uses for the "ground," or beginning, of the formation of the subject is "nature." And this "nature" of man, out of which he "develops" into a subject, is aesthetic: "aesthetic nature" ("Fourth Grove," 199). It is aesthetic because it is not—yet—clear: neither well defined and distinct nor sensible and confused; not cognition but "feeling"*; not a praxis but an "obscure mechanism of the soul" (194). "Aesthetic," in Herder, means "obscure." And an aesthetics that does "what its name declares" is an investigation of the obscure.[4] The program of an anthropological genealogy of the subject can be realized only as an aesthetics because aesthetics is the science of the obscure and because it is only on the basis of the obscure that we can gain an understanding of clarity, including and especially the clarity of sensible cognition.

One central argument for the reconception of anthropology as aesthetics or of aesthetics as anthropology is Herder's claim that the obscure mechanism of the soul is not merely the "beginning," the precondition for the formation of the subject, but its "ground" because it is the "permanent basis in the soul" ("Fourth Grove," 194). Having already seen that the subject and his faculties must be formed, Baumgarten frames this insight in the concept of practice. Baumgarten had also already seen that the formation in practice of the subject and the subject's faculties is not without preconditions. Indeed, in his *Aesthetics*, he places a section that treats "*connate natural aesthetics* [. . .], the natural disposition of the entire soul for beautiful cognition, with which one is born" (§28), before the section about practice. Nature, as the precondition *of* the subjective faculties, thus appears in Baumgarten solely as a natural predisposition *for* the subjective faculty—that is to say, not in fact as nature.

---

* "Away, then, with *cognitio*: Feeling constitutes a *genus* of its own" ("Baumgarten," 671).

Herder can therefore also frame the step that leads him beyond Baumgarten's aesthetics as follows:

> *Natural* aesthetics (like natural logic) differs from *artificial* aesthetics not merely by *degree* but in its *essence*; for the former is *always habitus*, but the latter, *scientia*; the former *operates* in *sensations* and *obscure* concepts; the latter *teaches* and *persuades* in *propositions* and distinct *concepts*: whence . . . *artificial* aesthetics has *evolved* out of *natural* aesthetics; which fact, then, must be liable to explanation based on *man*—as an *important* natural *phenomenon* in its *own right*. All men have *aestheticam connatam*, for they are *all born* as *sensible animals*. ("Baumgarten," 660)

In Herder, then, to speak of man's "aesthetic nature" as not merely the beginning of or the precondition for, but the ground of the soul means two things. First, it means thinking of the difference between aesthetic nature and the subjective faculties as a difference not merely of degree but of essence. (Herder makes this point in describing man's aesthetic nature in terms of its animal- and indeed plantlike beginnings.*) Second, it means insisting on aesthetic nature as the ground or basis of the subjectivity into which it develops precisely because of its essential difference from this subjectivity. These two aspects of Herder's aesthetic genealogy contradict both a teleological view, which sees man's nature as ordered toward the gestalt of his subjectivity formed in practice, and a merely external stratification of natural-aesthetic mechanisms and subjective-cognitive practices. Aesthetic genealogy or genealogical aesthetics means thinking of the subjective faculties as carrying within themselves, as their other, the obscure mechanism out of which they have arisen.

But what constitutes the "obscure mechanism of the soul"?

---

* "Let us start somewhere in the middle and return to the time when man first became a phenomenon of our world, when he emerged from a state of having been merely a thinking and perceiving vegetable and began to develop into an animal. Still he appears to be endowed with no sentiment other than the obscure idea of his ego, *as obscure as a vegetable might feel it*. Yet in this idea the concepts of the entire universe lie contained; from it, all of man's ideas evolve; all sentiments sprout forth from this vegetal feeling, just as in visible Nature the seed carries within it the tree and every leaf is an image of the whole" ("Fourth Grove," 194; translation modified).

FORCE AS EXPRESSION

To understand the obscure mechanism of the soul out of which emerge all faculties of the subject formed in practice, we must examine Herder's redefinition of the concept of force. In *On the Cognition and Sensation of the Human Soul: Observations and Dreams*—an essay that, despite its subtitle, contains Herder's most systematic treatment of the matter—he introduces the concept of force to explicate the programmatic endeavor of Leibniz's "monad-poem." The very same endeavor—"to explain even motion as an appearance of an *internal condition*"⁵—had led Baumgarten to the concept of the subject and its faculties. For Herder this "internal condition" is force (*Kraft*). He immediately adds that this reference to a force, also called a "power [*Macht*]," should not be understood as a conventional causal explanation: "I do not say that I hereby *explain* anything; I have not yet known any philosophy that explained what *force* is, whether force stirs in a single being or in two beings" (*Cognition*, 194). In fact, the concept of force is located on the same level as "space" and "time." It designates a form of apperception (not an object of apperception) that philosophy "always already *presupposes*" when it does what it does: "to *observe, order* together, *elucidate*" (194). The concept of force, then, designates not an event or an object but a "relation."⁶

The structure of this relation is an "operation [*Würkung*] of one thing *into* another" (*Cognition*, 194)—it is not an external effect of one thing *upon* the other. Instead, the other is that which is effected and engendered by the one, such that the one is transformed or continuously formed into the other ("the great secret of the *ongoing formation, renewal, refinement* of all beings" [188; translation modified]). The other, then, is the other of the one—*its* other—into which the one extends its existence because the disposition of the other is already contained in the one. "Force" means that the one and the other exist only in operation, in the transition of the one into the other, in the emergence of the other out of the one. Thus "force" also means that the one and the other are so closely interrelated that the other is the one in another form.

When Herder speaks of "expression," as he frequently does, what he is describing is this interrelation between the one and the other. "Expression" does not mean a relation between something internal and something external but, rather, an operational relation, union of the one and the other by virtue of a third contained in them. The other is expression. It is the expression of the one, which is force; however, the force whose expression is the other is the force whose expression the one also already was. The one, then, is not only force or expression—it is force *and* expression: the one is the expression of a force and, at the same time, the force whose expression is the other. The force exists only in expression, but the force is not merely any particular expression of itself; it is prior to and, hence, beyond any particular expression.[7]

THE OBSCURE MECHANISM OF THE SOUL

Herder's use of his expressive concept of force pervades his entire oeuvre.[8] For instance, in the first "Critical Grove," "dedicated to Mr. Lessing's *Laocoön*," Herder uses it to emend Lessing's rudimentary definition of action as a sequence of objects or parts: "[T]he concept of succession is only half of the idea of an action; it must be a *succession through force*; thus arises an action."[9] Yet the concept of action is, for Herder, only one case, not the paradigm, of succession through force. Action belongs to the domain of clarity, which cannot be understood in isolation but must be understood as grounded in the obscure. Here, too, in the domain of the obscure, the general form of "force" and "expression" applies. Yet in the domain of the obscure, "succession through force" is succession without consciousness—unconscious succession through an unconscious force. Herder's claim that the obscure, as "feeling," constitutes a "genre [genus]" separate from cognition (see footnote on p. 34) emphasizes the decisive point: Because the obscure is not conscious, it cannot be cognition, for, being unconscious, it is incapable of all normative distinction—such as that between appearance and truth—which applies in the domain of cognition. The succession through force, which constitutes the obscure mechanism of the soul, is an ongoing formation propelled by an internal principle, without any conscious relation to this principle as a norm of formation.

The difference of "genre [*Gattung*]" that begins to emerge between subjective faculty and unconscious obscure force becomes fully clear only when we represent to ourselves—with and against Herder—how the unconscious force of the soul can*not* be conceived: the unconscious obscure force is not a subjective faculty because it is not self-conscious and, hence, not normative. Yet this means neither that the unconscious obscure force is *mechanical* nor that it is *biological* because the obscure force knows neither law nor purpose. We can and must represent this to ourselves against Herder because he summons, in *On the Cognition and Sensation of the Human Soul,* models and metaphors that point in both directions—that of mechanics and that of biology. These models and metaphors, however, also prove inadequate to the attempt to grasp the obscure mechanism of the human soul: they cannot be sustained.

The obscure mechanism of the human soul is not mechanical: In *On the Cognition and Sensation of the Human Soul* and frequently in other works, Herder speaks of "mechanical" cause-and-effect relations. However, he also calls materialist attempts to explain the origin of the human soul "strangely mechanical dreams" (*Cognition,* 191) and describes initial obscure sensations as a "mechanical or super-mechanical play" (192). Herder often uses "mechanical" with respect to the unconscious forces of the human soul to mean what Leibniz described as the self-actuating effective automatism of the "active force": the active force "is . . . carried into action by itself and needs no help but only the removal of an impediment."[10] But Herder never uses "mechanical" with regard to the unconscious forces of the human soul to suggest that these forces and their effects are capable of a mechanistic explanation. Mechanistic explanations describe events as effects of forces in accordance with general laws. In this context, the mechanical concept of force explains the effect one body exerts upon another by the effect of the force of yet another body upon the first body, and so on. Force, mechanically understood, *is* "force of reaction, a force that a body 'exerts only in changes of its state produced by another force impressed upon it.'" Force, mechanically understood, is subject to the law of cause and effect between bodies and, thus, has calculable magnitude.[11]

If force in the mechanical sense is thus the cause behind the effect one body exerts *upon* another, Herder's expressive concept of force describes the process of the *generation* of forms: force, in the expressive sense, is the internal principle of the production of one form out of another, the "alteration" of one form into another, not of the alteration one body effects in another. Mechanistic explanations use the concept of force to explain, according to general laws, interactions between bodies that are external to these bodies. Herder rejects this model "of clumsy mechanism, wooden pressure and impact" (*Cognition*, 207) for the "obscure mechanism of the soul" because it misconceives the nature of the processes of the soul. Its sensations are "expressions," and forces of the generation of forms operate forever, and in forever new and different ways, in them. The processes of the soul have their own internal principles and are not subject to any external law.

The obscure mechanism of the human soul is not biological: where Herder, in *On the Cognition and Sensation of the Human Soul*, frames his critique of mechanistic thinking, the term "life" usually appears. For example, to say that the soul does not obey a "clumsy mechanism" means that, "according to all experiences, everything is full of irritation and *life*" (207). Herder uses "life" to designate an internal, "spiritual" bond between the elements:

> A mechanical or supermechanical play of expansion and contraction means little or nothing if its cause from within and without were not already presupposed: "*irritation, life*." The Creator must have linked a spiritual bond that certain things are similar to this sensing part, and others contrary to it—a bond which depends on no mechanism . . . (192)

Yet the concept of life is not limited to this idea of an internal, "spiritual" affiliation between a sensation and its object. Herder further writes regarding the lives of plants and animals:

> Observe that plant, that beautiful structure of organic fibers! How it twists, how it turns, its leaves to drink the dew that refreshes it! . . . If we were to see through the infinitely subtler and more complexly woven animal body, would we not likewise find each fiber, each muscle, each irritable part in the same function and in the same force, of seeking life-juice in its own way? (192)

Here, with reference to plants and animals, "life" designates not merely something "supermechanical" or "spiritual" but, rather, an internal connection or, more precisely, a purpose: the "same function and . . . the same force" of the plant or animal direct "each fiber . . . muscle and . . . part" toward the *purpose* for which they exist. This more precise and substantial definition of the concept of life corresponds to a methodological rupture in its employment. We can speak, Herder says initially, of "life" only in *"analogy to the human being"* (188). Life, then, exists in nature only to the extent that we "[enliven] everything with our sensation" (187).[12] At its origin, "life" is thus a psychological concept that is subsequently put to—largely uncontrolled—biological use. As the status of the concept of life shifts—from its psychological-analogical to its biological-objective use—so, what is more important, does its substance. Biologically conceived, "life" designates the immanent teleological totality of the organism; biologically conceived, what is alive is organized by teleology.* However, there is no path back from this biological concept of life to the psychological concept with which Herder had begun, the concept he had used to designate the "supermechanical" process of the human soul. The latter is, even in its "obscure ground" in the "life" of the sensations, not an organism. This means that the obscure unconscious force of the human soul is not a biological force. Both forces, the unconscious one of the soul and the biological one of the organism, differ from mechanical force in that both are internal principles of self-alteration or self-movement. Yet the biological force consists in an orientation toward a purpose within the totality of the life form of an organism. It is the force that serves the reproduction of this life form, the biological generality in each particular instance and specimen. The unconscious and obscure force of the soul, by contrast, does not serve the purposes of "generation," "nutrition," or "reproduction." It is unrelated to any form and does not serve any purpose.

These, then, are the three negations that define the "obscure mechanism of the soul": (1) The obscure force of the soul is *not subjective*: it is without normative substance. (2) The obscure force of the soul is *not*

---

* "[I]n all creatures, from man to the maggot and from the cedar down to mildew, there is a particular, innate effective drive, [which is] active throughout an individual's life, at first to take their destined shape; then, to maintain it; and, where it has suffered destruction, to reconstitute it if possible.

A drive (or a tendency or a *conatus*, however one may wish to call it) . . . that seems to be among the first causes of all generation, nutrition, and reproduction; and which I will here, to prevent all misinterpretation and to distinguish it from the other forces of nature, call the drive of formation (*nisus formativus*)." Blumenbach, "Über den Bildungstrieb" (n. 12), 249–50.

mechanical: it is not subject to an external law. (3) The obscure force of the soul is *not biological*: it does not have an organic purpose. From this triple negation emerges the definition of the obscure force of the soul: it is the conceptual elaboration of Descartes's indeterminacy hypothesis.

The obscure force of the soul is not like the practical faculties of the subject, and it is nonetheless neither one of the (mechanical) forces causing effects that govern the mechanical world of bodies nor one of the (biological) forces of reproduction, which define the living nature of organisms. The positive substance of the triple negation that characterizes the concept of the obscure force consists in the observation that the obscure force of the soul is neither subjective nor mechanical nor biological but *aesthetic*.

Herder conceives of philosophical anthropology as a genealogical regression into those times and forces when man was not yet a subject. He calls these forces of man "obscure," for they contrast with the practical and conscious faculties of the subject formed in practice. In this respect, they resemble mechanical and biological forces, which accounts for Herder's borrowings from mechanical and biological metaphors and models. Yet the "obscure force" of the soul is, even in Herder, not a *category* of mechanics or biology, for the obscure force of the soul neither exerts mechanical laws nor realizes biological purposes. It is without law or purpose—a category of aesthetics.

Genealogical anthropology, as aesthetic anthropology, thus leads back behind the subject. Yet it does not lead *beyond* man—into the world of mechanical bodies or living organisms—but *to* him. The "obscure force" is a presubjective and indeed countersubjective force that constitutes man. This is the fundamental definition of the aesthetic in and since Herder. The term "aesthetic" designates forces and modes of expression that are not subjective. Yet, at the same time, they are particular to man.

UNITY WITHOUT GENERALITY

The shared feature of the three conceptions of force from which the aesthetic concept of "obscure" force is distinguished consists in their relation, each in a different way, to one of the three basic forms of generality—a practical norm, a mechanical law, or a biological purpose. Indeed, a force (or a faculty) *is* the relation of some particular—a particular subject, a particular body, a particular organism—to the general. By virtue of its force, the particular is an agency—an agency of realization—of the general. For a subject, having a faculty means being able to realize the norms that define a praxis. For a body, having a mechanical force means being subject to laws of calculable interaction with other bodies. For an organism, having a biological force means being able to pursue the purposes that define its form of life. In all three cases, "faculty" or "force" designates the presence of the general in the particular. The general exists in the particular as force. By contrast, the triple negation that characterizes the obscure force as an aesthetic force describes it as a force that is not subject to the general and as a force without general content—without norm, law, or purpose. But what does the aesthetic force do? If it does *not* realize in its doing and exertion a general within the particular, how does aesthetic force exert itself?

According to Herder, the aesthetic force of the human soul operates as a "play of expansion and contraction" (*Cognition*, 192). The play of aesthetic force is a process in which we "receive, transform, and communicate" (196; translation modified), a process by which the soul can "receive and transform everything into itself" (206). Even though what is thus produced consists "not only of images [*Bilder*] but also of sounds, words, signs, and feelings," we "usually call the depth of this confluence *imagination* [*Einbildung*]" (204). The aesthetic force is the force of the imagination, and "imagination," according to Herder, means formation of *unity* [*Einheitsbildung*]. We see "in the case of each irritation, each sensation, each sense . . . that nature 'unites a manifold'" (209; translation modified). The fact that the imagination forms unity is traditionally understood to mean that the images it creates are conjunctions of independently given elements ("sensory impressions"). But then these impressions would have to exist prior to their imagination in the human soul. That is why Herder inverts this constellation: "Imagination," as the operation of the aesthetic force, is not the generation of images by the conjunction of impressions that precede them; it is the generation of images by their conjunction to other images. The imagination creates images by creating the unity of these images.

But here we continue on, [noting] that, however different this contribution of different senses to thought and sensation may be, in our inner selves everything flows together and becomes one. . . . From all
this, now, the soul weaves and makes for itself its robe, its sensuous
universe. (204–5)

Herder expresses the same idea in even more fundamental terms by
conceiving of the imagination (*Einbildung*) as "ongoing formation [*Fort-
bildung*]" (188; translation modified). Every act of imagination, of the
generation of an image, is an act of formation of unity because it is a
continuous transformation of one image into another; images are created not from impressions but from images. This metamorphic and
transformative process of imagination is the key to an understanding of
the aesthetic force: the generation of an image is the operation of a force,
and every image is thus the expression of a force. If all imagination is
thus ongoing transformation, then the generation of a new image is the
continuation of a previous generation; all operation of the force is an
ongoing, or *continuous*, operation. The operation of the aesthetic force of
imagination consists in creating an image as the expression of this force
and then continuing to operate, such that the first image morphs into a
second, which is another expression of the same force, and so on. Every
operation of the aesthetic force is a repetition of a previous operation.
The aesthetic force operates continuously, by repeating [*wiederholen*:
bringing again] itself and by replacing a self-generated expression of itself with another expression. *This* is why all imagination is an act of
formation of unity: because the *same* force operates in each instance.

Two facts demonstrate that no generality—no law, purpose, or
norm—regulates this process of the self-repetition of the aesthetic force:
(1) the various expressions of the aesthetic force disagree with one another, and (2) the expressions of the aesthetic force simultaneously reveal
and conceal it.

(1) Every operation of the aesthetic force is a repetition. An aesthetic
force operates by producing an expression, and then another and another.
If the aesthetic force is the force of its own repetition, if repeating itself is
what the aesthetic force does, then it has no end. The aesthetic force does
not stop in any of its expressions but goes beyond each one of them. By
repeating itself, the aesthetic force of imagination thus transcends each of

its expressions, replacing it with another. The expressions of the aesthetic force supersede and indeed contradict one another. Mechanical, biological, and practical forces have in common that every one of their effects is a particular realization of the same generality—the same law, the same purpose, the same norm. Every effect of a mechanical, biological, or practical force is thus equally valid, exemplifying the same general content and agreeing with one another. The expressions of the aesthetic force, by contrast, have nothing to agree on; they have no general content. As the same force operates continuously, one image metamorphoses into another. In the operation of the aesthetic force, to become means to become replaced.

(2) The aesthetic force is an endless generation and dissolution of expressions, an endless transformation of one expression into something different. Thus the operation of the aesthetic force consists in transcending, moment by moment, what it itself has produced. The aesthetic force creates new expression by voiding its previous expression. Mechanical, biological, and practical forces operate by producing a particular example of something general: an event determined by a law of mechanics; a movement that expresses a biological purpose; an action that achieves the good of a praxis. The operation of a mechanical, biological, or practical force is always complete in itself. The aesthetic force, by contrast, turns against its own expression, transforming it into another. The aesthetic expression is, therefore, as internally antagonistic as the aesthetic force itself. If the force is at once the creator and the destroyer, the expression of the force is matter and antimatter, content and chaos, the ground and the groundlessness of its expression. The expression of the force is also its concealment; the expression of an aesthetic force is "expression as though." In the operation of the mechanical, biological, practical force, something general—law, purpose, norm—realizes itself. In the operation of the aesthetic force, *nothing* realizes itself. The operation of the aesthetic force is a "spectacle [*Schauspiel*]" (*Cognition*, 187), a mere play[13] of expression and concealment.

———

ONLY IN ALLUSIONS, IN occasional hints and unintentional images, did Herder frame the idea of an aesthetic force without general content.

His treatise *On the Cognition and Sensation of the Human Soul* circles the idea, approaching it negatively by differentiating it from mechanics, biology, and praxis. Nowhere is his indirect approach more evident than when he rejects it in another domain—not the aesthetic but in the historical:

> Those who have so far undertaken to unfold the *progress of the centuries* have, for the most part, in the process, the pet idea: progress to *more virtue* and *happiness of individual human beings*. . . . Others, who *saw the objectionableness of this dream* and knew nothing better, saw *vices* and *virtues*, like climes, *change*, perfections, *arise* and *perish* like a springtime of leaves; human ethics and inclinations fly away, turn over, like *leaves of fate—no plan! no progress! eternal revolution—weaving and undoing!—Penelope-work!*[14]*

"AN INVALID OF HIS SUPERIOR FORCES"

In paragraphs five through twelve of his *Aesthetics*, Baumgarten discusses a number of objections that might be raised "against our science." The fourth objection is "that the sensible, imaginations, fairy tales, the confusion of the passions, etc., are unworthy of the philosopher and beneath his horizon" (*Aesthetics*, §6). This cannot be considered a paraphrase of Descartes's objection to a theory of sensibility, for Descartes did not maintain that the sensible is unworthy of philosophical scrutiny. Descartes's objection was, rather, that the sensible is *incapable* of such scrutiny. Baumgarten, however, rejects this objection by introducing a concept that makes a sharp distinction between aesthetics and rationalist philosophy—the concept of the human being:

> A philosopher is a man among men, and he would do well not to believe that such large a part of human cognition should be outside his purview. (*Aesthetics*, §6)

---

* "Homer's tale of Penelope, who in the evening unraveled what she had accomplished during the day, is a self-conscious allegory of art: What cunning Penelope inflicts on her artifacts, she actually inflicts on herself." Adorno, *Aesthetic Theory* (chap. 2, n. 19), 186–87.

Descartes's claim that, because of its indeterminacy, the sensible is un-knowable to philosophy is an immediate consequence of his rejection of the concept of the human being. The thought, "I am, I exist," inevitably gives rise to the question, "But who am I?" We cannot answer that question with the thought, "I am a human being," as this second thought would have to include "my body," "my life," and thus the sensible. Since I cannot know anything certain about these issues, I cannot, with certainty, call myself a human being.* Baumgarten, by contrast, justifies aesthetics precisely by reminding the philosopher that *he is a human being*. Baumgarten's justification of the enterprise of an ("aesthetic") scrutiny of the sensible consists in making the concept of the human being a fundamental concept of philosophical self-cognition.

Herder's objection to Baumgarten's aesthetics is that Baumgarten did not understand what he had gotten himself into with this hypothesis. For our "strength as human beings" consists "in the *ground* of our soul" (see p. 34), and the ground, or beginning, of our soul is constituted by obscure—not merely confused—forces, by "feeling" not cognition—by a play of expression without norm, law, or purpose. According to Herder, the "error" of Baumgarten's aesthetics is thinking of man as subject. Thinking aesthetically means thinking of man, but thinking of *the difference between man and subject*.

Herder's considerations of the obscure mechanism of the soul are seminal to avoiding Baumgarten's "error" because they allow us to think about the difference between man and subject without dualism. The modern dualism of nature and spirit compels us to conceptualize everything in man that is not subject as nature. Here, nature is taken in the sense of the modern natural sciences—initially, in the mechanical sense, then, since the eighteenth century, in the biological sense. The critical thesis contained in Herder's concept of obscure force is that if man is not—entirely—subject, it is not because he is nature in the mechanical or biological sense. Rather, man's nature is human nature—nature taken in the aesthetic sense: an obscure force whose

---

* "What then did I formerly think I was? A man. But what is a man? Shall I say 'a rational animal'? No; for then I should have to inquire what an animal is, what rationality is, and in this way one question would lead me down the slope to other harder ones, and I do not now have the time to waste on subtleties of this kind" (*Meditations*, II.5; 17).

operation consists in the play of its expression. Man is not—entirely—sub-ject because the obscure forces of his aesthetic nature, unlike the practi-cal faculties of the subject, do not realize a general form in the particular instance. Because man has an aesthetic nature, he forever lags behind his subjectivity—"an invalid of his superior forces."[15] Yet the grounds of man's inability ever to become subject in his entirety are also the grounds upon which he can become subject at all.

On the one hand, because man's aesthetic nature is obscure force, it cannot be conceived (in the Aristotelian sense) as his being disposed, let alone destined, to form subjective faculties. The obscure force, in its play of expression, is neither subjective nor practical, and the practical faculties of the subject are formed only in socializing practice exercises, which, imposed from the outside, interrupt the play of force. The "birth" of the subject is the invasion into man of something alien.*

On the other hand, precisely because man's aesthetic nature is ob-scure force, it cannot also be conceived (in the mechanical or biological sense) as the indifferent other next to and separate from his subjective faculties, whose formation in practice interrupts its play. For in its play of expression, the obscure force exposes man to an indeterminacy that liberates him from all law and purpose and thus renders him capable of forming practical faculties, that is, subjectivity. The very play of the expression of obscure forces that constitute man's "aesthetic nature" enables the formation in practice of practical faculties whose exercise is directed against its play.

By thinking of human beings in terms of their aesthetic nature, Herder thinks of the difference between man and subject, the differ-ence between obscure force and practical faculty. However, he also thinks of the difference *within* man, thinks of man *as* difference. In other words, he thinks of man's aesthetic nature as the ground and the groundlessness of the subject—the "two most extreme ideas of our hybrid humanity."[16]

---

* "This teaching, this sense of an alien which imprints itself in us, gives our thinking its whole shape and direction. Regardless of all seeing and hearing and inflow from outside, we would grope about in deep night and blindness if instruction had not early on thought *for us* and, so to speak, imprinted in us ready-made thought-formulas" (*Cognition*, 212).

CHAPTER FOUR

Aestheticization: The Transformation of Praxis

MAN'S NATURE IS AESTHETIC, because man's nature, the ground of his soul, consists in the play of obscure forces. This is the fundamental tenet of Herder's aesthetic anthropology. How does Herder know this? Obscure forces are essentially unconscious—which is why they are called "obscure"—whereas practical faculties are, just as essentially, self-conscious. Practical faculties include the knowledge of their normative substance, the general form of the praxis they realize. The knowledge of practical faculties, then, is reflective knowledge: we know about our practical faculties because we have them. The explicit, and even the philosophical, knowledge of faculties merely articulates the implicit practical knowledge within faculties. But this is not the case with the obscure mechanism of the human soul.

An aesthetic anthropology disagrees with the philosophy of subjectivity on the level of its content: rather than conceiving of man on the basis of his subjectivity, it conceives the subject on the basis of man. But an aesthetic anthropology must also conceive of itself in a different way: it cannot be the articulation of our practical self-consciousness, for in its genealogical regression into man's aesthetic nature, anthropology transcends the horizon of the subject and his self-conception.

Herder occasionally attempts to solve this problem by assigning responsibility for the anthropological knowledge of the "deep abyss of obscure sensations, forces, and irritations" to a psychology that would be "in each step determinate *physiology*" (*Cognition*, 196). In a physiological perspective, however, the obscure mechanism of the soul becomes an earlier stage, perhaps even a concealed stratum, to which we can gain access only by means of cognition from the outside.[1] Such a view is refuted by the fact that the obscure mechanism of the soul is impeded in its operation by practice and instruction—the "sense of an alien which imprints itself in us" (212). But it also continues to operate within us: it leaves a "first all-powerful impression" and "is never lost."[2] Man's "aesthetic nature" is not a concealed stratum far beneath his subjectivity, which he has left behind. On the contrary, it continues to exist, expressing itself, in interruptions and transformations in the subject and bringing itself to bear against the subject's practical faculties. That is how we know of man's original aesthetic nature: because it continually shows itself.

The question regarding the knowledge of man's aesthetic nature, then, can be answered only if the aesthetic is not merely "nature"—not merely an initial state, the other of "culture," which precedes it. If the aesthetic can be known, it must be because an "obscure mechanism" intervenes in the culture of practical subjectivity without, at the same time, becoming a component or trait of culture.[3] Man's aesthetic force *manifests itself* as an interruption of the rational subject and its practices in aesthetic events. We know of our aesthetic nature because we have experienced such events.

FROM ENTHUSIASM TO ENLIVENMENT

Aesthetic events are moments of the intrusion of man's aesthetic nature into his praxis, his subjectivity. If man's aesthetic nature constitutes the "beginning," the ground as much as the groundlessness, of his subjectivity, then the aesthetic event in which this beginning manifests itself is an act of regression into the play of obscure forces out of which and against which the subjectivity formed in practice has formed itself.

One influential model for a conception of the aesthetic as a lapse from subjectivity is presented in Plato's theory—or the theory cited by Plato—of poetic enthusiasm:

> For all the good epic poets utter all those fine poems not from art, but as inspired and possessed, and the good lyric poets likewise; just as the Corybantian worshippers do not dance when in their senses, so the lyric poets do not indite those fine songs in their senses, but when they have started on the melody and rhythm they begin to be frantic, and it is under possession—as the bacchants are possessed, and not in

their senses, when they draw honey and milk from the rivers—that the soul of the lyric poets does the same thing, by their own report. For the poets tell us, I believe, that the songs they bring us are the sweets they cull from honey-dropping founts in certain gardens and glades of the Muses—like the bees, and winging the air as these do. And what they tell is true. For a poet is a light and winged and sacred thing, and is unable ever to indite until he has been inspired and put out of his senses, and his mind is no longer in him.[4]

Poesy (*poiesis*)—according to Hans-Georg Gadamer's summary of the Platonic view—is "divine madness and possession" and is thus "in any case not *knowing*. It is not a skill (*technē*) which could account for and justify itself and its truth."[5] Poesy is not a practical performance, not an act; it is not based on a practical knowledge, not an ability. Hence poetry is not a practical work, not a good. Thus the series (and unity) of the Platonic objections. What takes place in poesy is a collapse of practical subjectivity.

Just like this Platonic model of poetic enthusiasm, aesthetics conceives of the opposition between the unconscious play of obscure forces and the conscious praxis of the rational subject. Yet even where aesthetics draws directly on Plato, as it does in the theory of genius, it is neither a mere Platonism nor even an inverse Platonism. It is not just the same description with inverted valorizations (for Plato's citation of the theory of poetic enthusiasm aims, of course, at a critique of the poets, who, as enthusiasts, are incapable of the truth). Although aesthetics, too, is concerned with the invasion of the play of obscure forces into the praxis of the rational subject, it conceives of the relation between obscure force and subjective praxis in a different way from the model of enthusiasm—and the difference is decisive. That the poets' utterances do not derive from their own knowledge and ability "from art" means, for Plato, that they are "possessed by one of the heavenly powers." In other words, "the poets are merely the interpreters of the gods" (*Ion*, 534c, e). That is what the poet's "enthusiasm" means: an exterior and alien—a higher—power speaks through him. The enthused poet is a "telephone of the beyond."[6]

Aesthetics, by contrast, describes the intrusion of the aesthetic into the subject as the operation of the subject's *own* obscure forces. The fundamental importance that Herder's aesthetic anthropology ascribes to learning,* to the subject's "genesis," implies that the play of the obscure forces and the subject's practical faculties are at once different and inseparably interrelated. The practical faculties emerge from the former, interrupting and transforming their play. Thus, the obscure forces that operate in the poet against his practical faculties are not only the other of those faculties but also their beginning. Whereas Plato conceives of poetic enthusiasm as the aggression of the divine into the subject, aesthetics conceives of the aesthetic as a regression of the subject into the state out of which and against which it has formed itself in practice.

That is why the aesthetic event is described as a "regression": it is a regression into aesthetic nature. And this event brings up the question, how—or by virtue of what—does this aesthetic regression take place? Plato's theory of poetic enthusiasm does not take up the issue of the causality of enthusiasm because the transformation of practical subjectivity into poetic mania is instilled "by one of the heavenly powers": the cause of this enthusiasm coincides with its content. Aesthetics, by contrast, requires a theory of aesthetic effect—a theory of the aesthetic regression into aesthetic nature as the effect of an aesthetic situation.[7]

What, then, brings about the subject's aesthetic regression into the play of its obscure forces? Johann Georg Sulzer, Herder's witness for the prosecution in his critique of an aesthetics "after the Baumgartian manner," replies: a transmission of "energy." In a note, Sulzer illustrates his use of the term "energy" as follows:

> I am compelled, for lack of another term, to use this word to indicate, most generally, a certain preeminent force not merely in speech but in all other things that appertain to taste. It is the very thing Horace (Serm. I. 4) calls *acer spiritus et vis in verbis et rebus*.[8]

Aesthetic "energy" consists in the "force" with which things "that appertain to taste" affect man. There are two other qualities belonging to things of taste that can also affect man: their "perfection" and their "beauty." "Energy" is distinguished from these two by the *mode* of its

---

* "Everything depends upon the distinction of *whether* we *learn the language*, or whether we *invent* it for ourselves." Herder, *Über die neuere deutsche Literatur. . . . Dritte Sammlung* (chap. 2, n. 2), 394; trans. "On Recent German Literature: Third Collection" (chap. 2, n. 2), 196.

effect: "The perfection we perceive in a thing calls upon us to reflect on it; beauty entrances us to behold or contemplate it; and energy engenders motion" (124). The energy of a thing—of a speech, an event, a sound—consists in its moving the soul.

These are stock ideas from the rhetorical tradition—like those to which Klaus Dockhorn refers in his observation that "modern aesthetics unfolds largely as an exercise in the interpretation of rhetorical writings, that is, as an endogenous history of intellectual development."[9] However, it is important to note *how* Sulzer reframes the rhetorical figure of the energy of motion ("pathos") by means of an aesthetic anthropology of force. Sulzer introduces the term *"Bewegung"*—meaning "motion" or "being in motion"—as the German complement of "emotion." This seems to imply that aesthetic energy affects the soul's feelings rather than its thinking. The same is suggested by two other terms Sulzer uses, *"reizen"* (to irritate, stimulate, charm) and *"rühren"* (to stir, move). One possible interpretation would be that—as Kant put it critically—a "sensation, which is [merely] the matter of an aesthetic judgment," becomes the "determining basis" of the aesthetic effect.[10] Kant thus takes aim at a conception of the aesthetic that explains the "motion" (or emotion) engendered in us by the things of taste, as an evaluation of the qualities of these things in our feeling or sentiment. Aesthetic motion, then, would be a strong reaction of feeling and, hence, a strong valuation of the qualities of an object. That Sulzer does *not* conceive of aesthetic motion in the fashion criticized by Kant, as a mechanism of affective evaluation, is demonstrated by his observation that aesthetic "energy" can affect not only "the soul's inferior forces" but equally "the manner in which we see or imagine things, that is, the soul's superior forces" ("Energie," 135). In other words, *all* "forces" of the soul, not merely our affects, can be "moved" by the energy of a word, an object, or a sound. All "forces" of the soul, the superior as much as the inferior ones, imagination and thinking as much as feeling, can be set in "emotion"—that is, in motion—by the aesthetic transmission of energy.

Here, then, is the first fundamental insight arrived at by a consideration of the aesthetic that inquires, beyond the definition of the aesthetic as man's original nature, into its manifestation in aesthetic events. "Aesthetic," in the sense delineated by Herder, still designates an operation, a play of forces that can also be called "obscure" because no general is realized in it. However, the quality of being aesthetic can now no longer be described as an initial stage of a fundamental stratum within man. In aesthetic events, the play of obscure forces invades the praxis of rational subjectivity and causes the subject to regress. In this aesthetic regression, in the play of these obscure forces, then, the subject does not simply return to his original state. The event of regression is more radical than that. Rather than coercing the practical faculties formed in practice to abdicate in favor of a state of forces at obscure play, the subject's aesthetic regression sets these very practical forces formed in practice in "motion," involving them in a play of obscure forces. To be set in "motion," to become "emotion," is a quality of the mode in which "forces" are exercised. Given a sufficient influx of energy, this modal quality can affect all aspects of the human soul—its "inferior" as much as its "superior" forces (Sulzer) or, in our terminology, its obscure forces as much as its practical faculties. The aesthetic regression is an aesthetic transformation of the practical faculties into forces at obscure play.

Sulzer's very terminology reflects this decisive insight. Whereas Herder frames his project of aesthetics in opposition to Baumgarten's by reconceiving Baumgarten's notion of the obscure, Sulzer uses Baumgarten's metaphors of liveliness to frame an idea that explodes Baumgarten's theory of sensible cognition (which had forcibly united liveliness and clarity; see p. 25). Sulzer speaks of "liveliness" as a quality of energetic words, objects, and sounds,[11] but, most important, as a modality of the soul as it is moved by this energy. The effects of aesthetic energy "[restore] to the soul its entire liveliness; what at first merely pleased now begins to stir [*rühren*] and to set in motion" ("Energie," 128). The aesthetic transformation of the soul, the regression of the subject into aesthetic nature, is an "enlivening" transformation of the practical faculties to the point where they become obscure forces and begin to play.

A FEELING FOR ONESELF

That man's original nature is "aesthetic," that this nature manifests itself in the subject in aesthetic events, that this aesthetic manifestation must be understood as a regression of the subject, that this aesthetic regression must thus be understood as a transformation, an "enlivenment," of the subject's practical faculties—this argument is the first step one can take using Sulzer's formulations concerning the "energy" of the aesthetic. A second step consists in a more detailed explication of the mechanism of aesthetic transformation-as-regression. This step, too, is suggested by Sulzer's considerations, as he describes the aesthetic effect that moves the soul:

> He who wishes to ome thoroughly acquainted with this cause [of "motion"] ought to recall those happy moments when the soul, giving itself over to gentle dissipation, engenders without compulsion or effort a series of delightful ideas. Like a stream whose water flows along imperceptibly, it does not feel its own industry; it forgets itself as it directs its entire attention to the varied painting created by the series of its ideas. Usually, this state does not last long; the slightest cause disrupts the pleasant deception. Then the soul turns its eyes away from this painting and toward itself, its state, the mode of its existence at the present moment. This change is always accompanied by a greater or lesser *perturbation*, which engenders movement. ("Energie," 124–25)

We cannot fail to hear in this description the echoes of Edmund Burke's distinction between the beautiful and the sublime, a distinction that Sulzer clearly understands not as a contrast between two types of the aesthetic but as a process, a "transition from the state of observation or contemplation" of the beautiful (cf. 124) "to that of motion" (128). Yet Sulzer draws on Burke not only for the similarities and differences between distinction and conjunction of two aspects of aesthetic effect—"contemplation" (of the beautiful) and "motion" (induced by the sublime)—but also and primarily for Burke's explanation of the sublime pleasure we take in the terrible. This pleasure, according to Burke, who in turn draws on discussions of the paradox of tragedy since Aristotle, raises the question, "how any species of delight can be derived from a cause so apparently contrary to it."[12] Burke sketches a solution to this problem as follows:

> [T]error is a passion which always produces delight when it does not press too close ... Whenever we are formed by nature to any active purpose, the passion which animates us to it, is attended with delight, or a pleasure of some kind, let the subject matter be what it will. (*Enquiry*, 42)

Sulzer reconceives Burke's "animation" of the soul as the "liveliness" of its forces. More important, Sulzer also highlights the operation, which, according to Burke's description, must take place so that the motion of the soul's forces as it faces the terrible can nonetheless induce a feeling of delight "when it does not press too close." The soul must change the direction of its attention, turning it away from the object and "toward itself, its state, the mode of its existence at the present moment" ("Energie," 125). The paradoxical pleasure of the sublime is predicated on an act of self-reflection.

This point is clearly described by Moses Mendelssohn in his "Rhapsody or additions to the Letters on sentiments."[13] Mendelssohn begins with a more exacting version of the problem of explaining the pleasure we take in the terrible. This difficulty, he writes with reference to Descartes, arises from the fact that "all pleasant sentiments originate in the observation of an object as something perfect,"[14] whereas the terrible objects of the sublime are devoid of all perfection and even good qualities. Mendelssohn maintains that the way out of this dilemma, which is likewise suggested by Descartes,* consists in the insight that, against all appearances, the pleasure in the terrible is not in fact a pleasure in its object at all:

> To be sure, like the will, pleasure is based on nothing else but a genuine or [an] apparent good. But this good may not always be sought in the object outside us, in the original picture [Urbild]. Even the deficiencies and evils of the object can, as representations, as determinations of the thinking projection, be good and pleasant. ("Rhapsody," 137)

The "thinking projection," whose "representations" of the "deficiencies and evils of the object" can in themselves be "pleasant," is (according to Mendelssohn's version of Baumgarten's new terminology) that "substance" which is the "subject" of these very representations. Terror—and thus the terrible—is pleasant when we experience it as our passion, as

---

* There is, distinct from the "enjoyment [the soul] has of the good," a "purely intellectual joy which comes into the soul by the action of the soul alone, and which can be said to be a delightful excitation, excited in it by itself." Descartes, *The Passions of the Soul* (n. 14), 91; 69.

the "motion" of our soul. When we take pleasure in the terrible, we establish a "distance" (*Enquiry*, 36), "separating the relation to ourselves from the relation to the object" or, conversely, "the objective from the subjective" ("Rhapsody," 138, 136). When we take pleasure in the terrible, the soul reflexively turns its attention to its own state rather than the state of the object of its experience. Incited by the terribleness of the object, the soul thus finds itself in a state of excitement. Furthermore, this observation is accompanied by a feeling of pleasure, for it contains a judgment of goodness or perfection precisely as demanded by the Cartesian definition of pleasure. Only now it is not the perfection of the object, which is being experienced, but that of its subject—the perfection that consists in nothing other than this state of the soul, its being excited, moved, and active. For the soul, according to Mendelssohn's version of Dubos's insight, "longs merely to be moved, even [if] it is to be moved by unpleasant representations" ("Rhapsody," 137). The fulfillment of this longing, of this striving to be stirred by whatever means—even the representation of terrible objects—is what constitutes our pleasure in these objects.

How must we conceive of self-reflection so that we can understand it as Mendelssohn's answer to the question of why we take pleasure in the terrible? We must conceive of it as a specifically aesthetic self-reflection. This implies that we must not confuse it with philosophical self-reflection, which it resembles to such a degree that aesthetic self-reflection was subsequently often compared to the "transcendental" reflection of philosophy.[15] But the difference between the two is fundamental. Philosophical self-reflection inquires into the conditions that enable successful praxis. Such praxis is structured as the realization of the general (the general form of a praxis) in the particular (the individual instance in the here and now). Philosophical self-reflection aims at an exploration of human faculties. Such faculties can be the objects not only of cognition but also of experience, and the experience of human faculties can be accompanied by pleasure. In philosophical self-reflection, the pleasure we take in ourselves is the pleasure we take in the practical faculty that constitutes human subjectivity, that is, in the good that is the faculty that enables a good.

By contrast, the experience of the terrible, the "terror" (as Burke would have it) of the sublime, consists precisely in the failure of our faculties, in our inability to act. And yet we experience pleasure. However, this also cannot be effected by our lack of faculty, our inability to act, our failure, for these cause us unmixed displeasure. The state in which we experience terrible objects with pleasure is thus neither a state of faculty nor the lack of faculty—neither the ability nor the inability to act. It is a different state altogether, one that eludes the conventional alternatives of success or failure. Like philosophical self-reflection, in this other state the human soul perceives itself in a different sort of relation to itself—a relation in which the attention is directed toward something we ordinarily, in the modes of cognition or volition (or even "contemplation"), "forget" ("Energie," 125). In this sense, it is a reflective relation to the self. We direct our attention to ourselves, to our faculties. But we do not direct it to them *as* faculties, and in the aesthetic relation to the self, we do not relate to ourselves as subjects. If we did so, we could not but experience our powerlessness and lack of faculty in the face of the terrible with displeasure. Instead we relate to our faculties beyond the alternatives of ability or inability, of success or failure.

The aesthetic relation to the self undertakes an "abstraction."[16] It relates to the faculties of the soul as *separate* from what they are (good) for; it relates to the faculties purely as such, without regard to their practical purpose and normative content. Yet this separation of the faculties from their good is something the aesthetic self-reflection does not find in place but, in fact, engenders; it exists only in and by virtue of aesthetic self-reflection. Thus, aesthetic self-reflection is that act which separates not only the subjective from the objective but also the faculty from the good, from praxis. Yet the subject's faculty exists only in this interrelation; a faculty without normative content and practical purpose is not a faculty. Aesthetic self-reflection leads to the disintegration of the unity of the faculty, the agency of the subject. What remains is man's aesthetic nature, the play of obscure forces.

———

MENDELSSOHN AND SULZER DESCRIBE the aesthetic as an event—the event of an aesthetic effect upon the human soul. In doing so, each of them focuses on one of two interrelated aspects. In analyzing the pleasure we take in the terrible, Mendelssohn describes the mechanism of self-reflection by which subjective faculties are isolated and separated from the practical relations in which they are embedded. Using terms such as "motion [*Bewegung*]," "emotion [*Rührung*]," and "enlivenment [*Belebung*]," Sulzer describes how practical faculties are transformed back into obscure forces. Aesthetic self-reflection is a negative operation upon the practical faculties; in positive terms, its positive complement is the aesthetic transformation of the practical faculties into obscure forces at play.

The interrelated concepts of "enlivenment" and "self-reflection" describe the aesthetic effect *upon the human soul* not only as an event but also as a process *within the human soul*—a process in which practical faculties are transformed, by virtue of their own self-reflection, into obscure forces at play. This is the aesthetic process: the process of the transformation of the practical through its self-reflection. A praxis realized by faculties consists of particular instances that repeatedly enact a general form. As the faculties are turned back upon themselves, severed from their general content, and turned into forces, this practical totality is transformed. It becomes a sequence of expressions of a force that, in a state of heightened and enlivened motion, passes beyond and transcends any one of its expressions. In other words, it becomes aesthetic.

BECOMING AESTHETIC

Under the titles of "enlivenment" and "self-reflection," Sulzer and Mendelssohn define features of the aesthetic that have remained fundamental to aesthetic theory. No less fundamental, however, is the new conception of its ontology—the mode of being of what is called "aesthetic"—derived from Mendelssohn's and Sulzer's descriptions of the aesthetic as a process. In Herder, "aesthetic" designated a state of the soul, a mode of its operation. This state was defined by the typological opposition between the obscure and the clear, between sentiment and cognition. In describing the interrelation between the obscure and the clear as both rupture and development, Herder reformulates this typological opposition in temporal terms. However, because he consistently thinks of the aesthetic state as original, the sense of process remains external to it. In other words, there *was* once an aesthetic (natural) state of obscure forces at play. This changes fundamentally with Mendelssohn and Sulzer because, although they insist with Herder (against Baumgarten's homogenization of the two) on the structural opposition between the aesthetic and the practical, they begin not with the original aesthetic state but with the present, practical state. As a result, the aesthetic is not a state but an event, and the event is a process. But an event that is a process is an event that remains in process, in the process of its occurring. If the aesthetic consists in the event of a self-reflective transformation of the practical, then it also exists *only* in the performance of this transformation. Only in this performance is it present. The aesthetic is not a being, an existent state of being, but a becoming; the aesthetic exists only as an aestheticization of the nonaesthetic.

But what does it say about the nonaesthetic, the practical, that it *can* be aestheticized? Aestheticization, as a transformation of the practical effected by its self-reflection, is not an external operation. The process of aestheticization reveals that the practical is, in fact, always in transition into the aesthetic: any totality that constitutes a praxis can become aesthetic when it reflects upon itself and is thus set in motion and enlivened. But once again, why is that so? The practical can *become* aesthetic because it *was* aesthetic.

The practical agent, the subject with his faculties, has not always been; he originated in the aesthetic, in the operation of obscure forces, and has come into being. This process is profoundly ambiguous and internally antagonistic. On the one hand, the formation of faculties in practice is predicated on the indeterminacy of the aesthetic force—what distinguishes it from the mechanical and biological forces and constitutes its "play" (see p. 37)—for this indeterminacy is man's, enabling him to become something else, a "subject." On the other hand, the normative order of the practical sphere must be imposed from the outside, asserted against the way the aesthetic force operates; the primal scene of subjectivation is the impression or internalization of an alien sense. Both aspects together define the emergence of the practical agent as a process of the transformation of the aesthetic. The practical subject emerges by drawing on the aesthetic forces already operating in him *and* suppressing their operation. Practical faculties were aesthetic forces that were directed against themselves. The transition of the practical into the aesthetic is possible only because it is a regression of the practical into the aesthetic—a return to what the practical faculties once were and what, though latent, continues to operate within them. And (only) because practical faculties were aesthetic can they become aesthetic: the transition of the practical into the aesthetic is possible because it is a regression of the practical into the aesthetic. Even, and especially, as a self-reflective transformation, then, is the aesthetic transformation of the practical an act of regression—a return to what the practical faculties once were and what, though latent, continues to operate within them.

Yet even if the aesthetic transformation—by self-reflection—of the practical is conceived as aesthetic regression, we still cannot do without the concept of the aesthetic state. The aesthetic is not a state, and there is no present in which it exists as a state. Rather, it is the *process of the aestheticization of the practical*. Yet the process of aestheticization also relates to a state of obscure forces at play within which and against which the practical faculties began. Without the "pastness" of this state, there can be no process of aestheticization. Herder has called—and up to now I have followed him in calling—this original obscure state of forces at play an "aesthetic" state, and this is the sense in which we must now understand that term. The aesthetic is not the state of the operation of obscure forces; it is not the original natural state of the human soul before the formation in practice of practical faculties. When there was an original obscure state of forces at play, this state was not yet aesthetic. The becoming-aesthetic of the practical is thus also the becoming-aesthetic of the other of the practical, the obscure. This state is aesthetic because, and to the extent that, it is brought about by the aestheticization of the practical and the reactualization of the obscure. Aestheticization is always a double process: the aestheticization of both the practical and the obscure.

LOOKING AHEAD: AESTHETIC THEORY

The process of aestheticization aims at undermining the social praxis by which objects are defined. The mechanism of this aesthetic undermining consists in a self-reflection of the very faculties through which the subject performs the praxis of determining. We should note that, unlike philosophical self-cognition, aesthetic self-reflection is not a subjective act.

It is not an act of reflection in which a subject assures himself of his faculties, for the obscure forces at play into which aesthetic self-reflection transforms the faculties of the subject do not belong to the subject. Nonetheless, they are *someone's* forces—not in the sense that a subject consciously and purposely exercises them in the way he exercises faculties—but in the sense that I experience their unfolding as my own, for it changes, "enlivens" me. In the process of aestheticization, then, a self-transformation takes place. The subject, the participant in and performer of social practices, transforms himself into the self as the agency of obscure forces at play.[17]

That the aesthetic and, hence, aesthetics are all about the self, its experience and transformation, is an objection that is almost as old as aesthetics. Hegel and Kierkegaard raised it against the romantics; Heidegger and Gadamer, against their radicalization in aestheticism. According to this critique, the attention to the aesthetic, in theory and praxis, appears as the expression of a purely self-centered subject—one who turns away from praxis, which is always social, and closes himself off toward objects that are disclosed to us only in the social practices that define them. The aesthetic, therefore, is about nothing but the pleasurable experience of man's "inner" state. Aesthetics is a discourse—matched by a praxis—of "subjectivization":

> Falling back upon the state and condition of man, upon the way man stands before himself and before things, implies that now [in the "modern age" and its aesthetics, CM] the very way man freely takes a position toward things, the way he finds and feels them to be, in short, his "taste," becomes the court of [jurisdiction] over beings. In metaphysics that becomes manifest in the way in which certitude of all Being and truth is grounded in the self-consciousness of the individual ego: *ego cogito ergo sum.* . . . I myself, and my states, are the primary and genuine beings. Everything else that may be said to be is measured against the standard of this quite certain being. My having various states—the ways I find myself to be with something—participates essentially in defining how I find the things themselves and everything I encounter to be.
>
> Meditation on the beautiful in art now slips markedly, even exclusively, into the relation to man's state of feeling, *aísthēsis*. (*Nietzsche*, I, 83; translation modified)

It is obvious in which respect this critique misunderstands aesthetics and its conception of the aesthetic. It fails to recognize the categorical difference and, hence, the double process (as reflection and regression) between faculty and force. It presumes that the aestheticization of praxis is a subjective act—an act in which the subject relates to himself; an act that a subject performs and in which he assures himself of himself. From Hegel to Gadamer, the critique of aesthetics as a "subjectiviza-tion" (a subjectivization of the beautiful, of art, of culture) thus misses precisely what has defined aesthetics since Herder's critique of Baumgar-ten: the fact that it calls the subject in question in the name of force.

Yet the objection to aesthetics remains that it conceives of the aesthetic—that is, the process of aestheticization—exclusively as the medium of a radically altered experience of *self*—and that it considers "the world [as nothing but] an occasion"[18] for such self-aestheticization. Baumgarten is immune to this objection, for by conceiving of the aes-thetic as a form of cognition, he also conceives of it as engaged in a de-terminative relation to objects. With Herder's critique of an aesthetics "in the Baumgartian manner," however, the aesthetic loses its determi-native object-relation. Does this render the aesthetic objectless—a self-reflective and lively play of obscure forces that runs its course—without any relation to the objects of experience?

The positions of an aesthetics of force that we have examined so far are unhelpful when they attempt to say how the process of aestheticiza-tion relates to objects. Sulzer vaguely suggests that the object is the "cause" of the disruption of the "pleasant deception" that elicits the pro-cess of aesthetic self-reflection ("Energie," 124). Mendelssohn describes the object of aesthetic representations in purely negative terms: "the ob-jective side of the representations must be weakened, set at some dis-tance, or moderated and obscured by neighboring concepts" ("Rhapsody," 137) for aesthetic self-reflection and self-pleasure to take place. Kant describes this cancellation of the object in an aesthetics of force by not-ing that "what I do with this presentation within myself" matters for the "enlivenment" of the faculties in the aesthetic performance of ide-ation, "not the [respect] in which I depend on the object's existence" (*CJ*, §2, B6; 46; translation modified). The reason is clear: there can be noth-ing about the object, defined as it is by recognizable qualities, that elicits the process of aestheticization, for it acquires these qualities only in the praxis of recognition, which the process of aestheticization undermines. Yet at the same time—hence the sense of frustration—this undermining of the determinative object-relation cannot amount to mere objectlessness, an absence of the object, any more than the aesthetic undermining of the practical subject amounts to selflessness. In the aestheticization of the praxis of determining, both elements, the subject and the object, are transformed equally and simultaneously. Even though the aestheticization of the praxis of determining cannot be engendered by specific qualities of an object, it does not take place simply "as a result of the prompting of the given presentation" of an object (*CJ*, §9, B31; 63). Rather, the transformation (transformation-as-regression) of subjective faculties into forces at obscure play transforms the recognizing determination of the object into a *different sort* of relation. To the aesthetic self-transformation, the world is not a mere "occasion and opportunity" (Carl Schmitt) because this self-transformation is possible only as the experience of the aesthetically transformed object.

The aesthetics of the obscure thus makes us consider the play of force as *representation* (*Darstellung*): the representation of the experience of an object. That is impossible within the framework defined by the traditional concept of representation, which underlies Baumgarten's concept of aesthetics. For there, representation is tied to cognition: "*Darstellung*" is a conjunction of ideational elements that expresses a perhaps indefinable—that is, "confused"—but nonetheless recognizable idea of an object. Representations, on the other hand, have a definable cognitive content. The aesthetics of the obscure removes the conceptual basis for this idea of representation because the aesthetic play of force undermines the praxis of determining and recognizing. In an aesthetics of the obscure, then, "representation" and "cognition" must be separated. Aesthetic representation must be thought of as representation without cognition, without a defined object.

What thus appears as an internal contradiction within the concept of "aesthetic representation"—between the terms "aesthetic" (a play of force) and "representation" (the experience of an object)—constitutes the core of what, since the decisive departure from Baumgarten's aesthetics of cognition, has been called "aesthetic theory." Aesthetic theory is the theory of aesthetic representation.[19] And its fundamental questions are: How and why is the aesthetic play of force suddenly transformed into the representation of an object? What is this object? And how does it appear to us at this moment of transformation? These questions lead into two areas—an aesthetic theory of the beautiful (natural) *thing* and an aesthetic theory of the beautiful *work* (of art)—that lie beyond the perspective of an aesthetic anthropology. And I will touch on them only briefly here.

(1) In the aesthetic play of force, one expression both creates and replaces another expression. Nothing, then, can be represented in the aesthetic play of force but this play itself. This is the core of what critics from Hegel to Gadamer have lamented as the objectless relation to the self of the aesthetic. Schiller put it as follows: "Man's imagination has, like his bodily organs, its free movement and its material play, in which, without any reference to shape, it simply delights in its absolute and unfettered power."[20] This leads Schiller to conclude that only a "leap" out of the play of force can lead to the emergence of form and, hence, representation of shape and content. The aesthetic play of force becomes representational by virtue of a counterimpulse, which can be given only by "a wholly new force" (ibid.) from the outside. However, in fact, it is performed by nothing other than the force against which the aesthetic play is directed. For the aesthetic play is not a state existing before, beside, or above the praxis of determining but is the process of the aestheticization of this praxis. It occurs on and, hence, against this praxis of determining. It has, in this praxis, an antagonist to which it remains related. Aesthetic representation is sparked in the antagonism between determinative praxis and play of force. The aesthetic play of force is directed against a recognizing determination of the object—but not by replacing this determination with another. Instead, it renders this determination itself an expression of a force and, thus, *in itself* undetermined. "Aestheticization" means: rendering undetermined. This is how the object becomes beautiful: the aesthetic play shows the object as a beautiful thing. Beautiful things are objects rendered undetermined in the play of force.*

---

* "The paradoxes of aesthetics are dictated to it by its object: 'Beauty demands, perhaps, the slavish imitation of what is indeterminable in things.'" Adorno, *Aesthetic Theory* (chap. 2, n. 19), 94; Adorno quotes Paul Valéry; see Valéry, *Œuvres* [Pléiade], vol. 2, ed. Jean Hytier (Paris: Gallimard, 1960), 681.

(2) The beautiful as the indeterminable enters representation by virtue of the aestheticization of the praxis of determining in the aesthetic
play. This is true of both beautiful things and beautiful works. The
aesthetic concept of the work of art is that of a structure that exists only
in the aestheticization of the praxis of determining, in the aesthetic play
of force. Yet beautiful works are not only like beautiful things, which
appear in the process of the aestheticization of determining. Unlike beautiful things, beautiful works also show the process of aestheticization.
The work of art is a representation, which, according to Friedrich Schlegel, "in all its descriptions [*Darstellungen*]" describes itself [*sich selbst mit
darstellt*].[21] What the work of art "describes" in each "description"—what
it corepresents in its aesthetic representation—is the process of aestheticization in which it represents itself, that is, the process from praxis and
its determinative faculties to the play of forces. This description-in-
each-description of aestheticization itself occurs in aesthetic fashion: not
by being told but by being shown. In other words, the work of art represents aestheticization by aestheticizing the representation. As a representation of aestheticization, that is, of the process from the praxis of
determining to the play of forces, the work of art is a representation of
the praxis of determining itself—a representation of the praxis of determining that already sees the play of forces operating within that praxis.
In the aesthetic perspective, the work of art is a complex operation with
a threefold representation: (a) Like the beautiful thing, the beautiful
work represents itself in the aesthetic play of forces. (b) Unlike the beautiful thing, the beautiful work represents the process of aestheticization
in which it represents itself with each of its representations. (c) The
beautiful work is at once both a new and an altered representation of
the practices of determining whose aestheticizing undermining it describes with each description.

CHAPTER FIVE

Aesthetics: Philosophy's Contention

THE FIRST PARAGRAPH OF Baumgarten's *Aesthetics* frames the task of conceiving Descartes's domain of "sensibility" in positive terms—as the domain of both a particular and a legitimate form of cognition, *cognitio sensitiva*. "*Aesthetics*," Baumgarten writes, "(theory of the liberal arts, science of the lower cognitive faculties, art of thinking beautifully, art of the analog of reason) is the science of sensible cognition." Here, he not only combines *theoria* and *ars*, examination and instruction, he also connects—and this is programmatic—the "lower cognitive faculties," the "analog of reason," with the "liberal arts" and the "art of thinking beautifully." Aesthetics, both in examining and in instructing, aims at sensible perception and presentation in general *as well as* their individual artful or beautiful performances. It integrates the particular theories of the arts and of the beautiful with the general science of cognition.

This integration is of central importance to Baumgarten's conception of philosophical aesthetics; it is the law determining the movement of aesthetics as a philosophical discipline—the dialectic of the particular and the general that keeps it in motion. In his "Meditations on Knowledge, Truth, and Ideas," Leibniz had pointed to "painters and other artists" as evidence for the claim that we can know something without being able to define it. Baumgarten makes a similar point: he learns from the aesthetic practice through which we become familiar with the arts that (and why) the rationalist opposition of sensibility and reason, conceived as causal mechanism and our own activity, respectively, is false. Aesthetic practice, he explains, teaches us that (and how) we are, in sensibility, "subjects." The meditation on the praxis of artists thus changes the fundamental philosophical terms in which an epoch articulates its self-conception. Baumgarten practices aesthetics as a critique of the prevailing philosophy by reflecting on the liberal arts and on beautiful thinking.

Baumgarten's conception of aesthetics as the dialectical interrelation of a general theory of sensibility with the particular theories of the arts and of the beautiful is predicated on his identifying, in the move that initiates his program, the entire field of aesthetics as the domain of "sensible cognition." The aesthetic dialectic of general and particular can unfold only within a homogeneous aesthetic field. By contrast, the distinction between force and faculty in the aesthetics of the obscure leads to a conception of the aesthetic, not as a particular species of sensible cognition but—as Herder would have it—as a categorically different "genre [*Gattung*]" *in opposition to* it. An aesthetics of the obscure thus dissolves the dialectical interrelation that, in an aesthetics "in the Baumgartian manner," integrates the general theory of sensibility with the particular theories of the arts and of the beautiful.

But what takes the place of this dialectic in an aesthetics of the obscure? And what takes the place of the act of critique—the critique of the prevailing philosophy through a reflection on the arts—that was grounded in the aesthetic dialectic of general and particular?

FROM PERFECTION TO SELF-ASSURANCE

The dialectic between the general theory of sensible cognition and the particular theories of the liberal arts or of beautiful thinking described in Baumgarten's *Aesthetics* is governed by the law of exemplariness: beautiful thinking and the liberal arts present exemplary realizations of a fundamental feature of all sensible cognition. They are "exemplary" in a double respect: First, they are—and they offer—an example. Second, because they are heightened forms of sensible cognition, they exhibit sensible cognition in general. They are the "perfect" sensible—in contradistinction to the imperfect, or the ordinary sensible.* The ordinary

---

* "Now since presentation can be either of an unperfected or of a perfected character, it will be the concern of general rhetoric or of general poetics, respectively. General rhetoric may be defined as the science which treats generally of unperfected presentation of sensate representations, and general poetics as the science which treats gener-

formations of the sensible share the fundamental features that define it. Yet, unlike the perfect formations, they do not exhibit these general features but, rather, conceal them.

The perfect formations of the sensible—the liberal arts and beautiful thinking—demonstrate an elevated possibility of sensibility that lets us see the reality of the sensible in a different way, as containing this possibility within itself. This is the case not because the ordinary performances of sensibility are, in truth, just like (or ought to become like) those special—beautiful or artful—performances. Rather, it is because the special, perfect performances bring to our attention a fundamental trait of sensibility, which is also true of its ordinary performances, that consists in the indefinability of the contents of sensible perception and representation. The fact that the special forms of sensible perception and representation exist and that they are adequate perceptions and representations of their object in its "material perfection" (*Aesthetics*, §561) demonstrates the conjunction of indefiniteness (or "confusion") and cognitive capability (or "clarity"), which defines the sensible in general. Beautiful or artful performances of sensibility can be called "exemplary" because they employ this fundamental defining feature in an extraordinary and elevated fashion in order to present surprise and novelty.* But this fundamental defining feature is also manifest in its ordinary formations of sensibility.

---

ally of the perfected presentation of sensate representations. The one is divided into sacred, profane, judicial, demonstrative, deliberative forms, and so on; the other, into epic, dramatic, lyric forms, with their sundry analogous species. But philosophers may leave the division of these arts to rhetoricians, who implant historical and experimental knowledge of them in the minds of their students. The philosophers should be busy in general in drawing boundary lines and especially in defining accurate limits between poetry and ordinary eloquence. The difference is, to be sure, only a matter of degree; but in the relegation of things to one side or the other, it requires, we think, no less capable a geometer than did the frontiers of the Phrygians and the Mysians" (*Poetry*, §CXVII; 78–79).

* "[T]hat kind of simile also, of which I spoke in treating of arguments, contributes to the ornament of style and helps to render it sublime or florid or attractive or striking. The more distant, indeed, the subject is from which any illustration is drawn, the more novelty it has, and the more surprise it causes." Baumgarten (*Aesthetics*, §741) quotes Quintilian (*Institutes of Oratory*, 8.3.74).

Exemplariness is a three-part constellation that relates the sensible, in general, and its two asymmetrical forms, the ordinary and the perfect formation. By insisting, against Baumgarten, on the generic distinction of the aesthetic as the obscure, Herder also dissolves this constellation of exemplariness. The step from an aesthetics of the faculty of sensible cognition to an aesthetics of the obscure force, then, does not only consist in a redefinition of the exemplary formations of the sensible, the liberal arts, and beautiful thinking, for the aesthetic as an unfolding of the play of obscure forces is no longer the particular instance of something general—no longer the perfect and, hence, exemplary realization of the fundamental defining feature of sensible cognition in general. Instead, the aesthetic consists in a process of aestheticization in which the practical faculties of sensible cognition are transformed and heightened such that they begin to play. The aesthetic play of force, then, does not realize the praxis of sensible cognition in either an ordinary or a perfect fashion. Nor does it manifest the general constitution of the praxis of sensible cognition. The aesthetic play of force neither exemplifies nor is exemplary of the praxis of sensible recognition. Rather, it turns the praxis of sensible cognition into something else altogether.

In Baumgarten, exemplariness, the category of "the sensible (in general)" spans the difference between the degree of perfection that separates the ordinary from the artful formation of the sensible. The aesthetics of force explodes this conjunction. If force and faculty are different genres and not species of one and the same sensibility, the aesthetic appearance of obscure force cannot be an "exemplary" manifestation of what force and faculty have in common. Something nonetheless becomes manifest in the aesthetic appearance of obscure force. Because the aesthetic play of obscure force unfolds in its aestheticization out of and against the practical faculties, it also lets us experience our practical faculties in a new and different way. The aesthetic experience of the play of force is the medium of a transformed experience of ourselves—a transformed experience of our own practical faculties.

That the aesthetic experience of the play of force is the medium of an experience of self is something Mendelssohn (influenced by Burke's phenomenology of the sublime) already noted: the transformation of faculties into force, their being set in "motion (*emotion*)" (as Sulzer put it), is associated with a feeling of pleasure one takes in oneself, in one's own state of lively motion. Mendelssohn limits the aesthetically pleasurable experience of self to this phenomenon: aesthetic pleasure flows solely from the experience of being in a state of lively forces at play. By contrast, Kant, in his *Critique of Judgment*, offers an interpretation of the aesthetically pleasurable experience of self that transcends that limitation and relates it again to the practical faculties whose enlivenment into force the self enjoys.

Following the aesthetics of the obscure, Kant likewise departs from Baumgarten's integration of beautiful and artful performances into the comprehensive domain of sensible cognition. The term "aesthetic" designates a specific way of performing the act of representation, which is neither cognitive nor determinative but "reflective." Kant further explains this aesthetic reflection as involving an "enlivenment of the two powers (imagination and understanding) to an activity that is indeterminate but, as a result of the prompting of the given presentation, nonetheless accordant" (*CJ*, §9, B31; 63; translation modified). Because our forces are "enlivened" and "in free play" (B28; 62; translation modified) in the aesthetic performance, aesthetic pleasure can then be defined as the way in which we "become conscious" (B30; 63) of this enlivenment of our cognitive forces. It is *by virtue of* the aesthetic pleasure we make for ourselves in our aesthetic reflection that we are conscious of ourselves and of the enlivened and heightened state of our forces in free aesthetic play. Aesthetic pleasure is, thus, the "sensation of . . . the facilitated play of the two mental powers (imagination and understanding) enlivened by their reciprocal harmony" (B31; 63; translation modified). Aesthetic pleasure is the medium of a relation to the self—yet it is "aesthetic" (through "mere inner sense and sensation") and not "intellectual" (through "consciousness of [our] intentional activity") (B30; 63).

To the question of why we experience the enlivenment of our forces with pleasure rather than with displeasure (or any other feeling), Mendelssohn offers a circular answer: the fact that we take pleasure in the enlivenment of our forces demonstrates that we regard the enlivenment of our forces as a good, which, in turn, shows that such enlivenment is something our soul "longs for." In other words, the enlivenment of our forces is pleasurable because enlivenment constitutes the "very essence" of our forces.* Kant, by contrast, gives a real answer to the question regarding the source of aesthetic pleasure by explaining what it teaches us about ourselves. When we take pleasure in the aesthetic enlivenment of our forces, we learn that we have practical faculties. The pleasure of aesthetic enlivenment, then, expresses not a mere self-affirmation based on the "very essence" of our forces, in other words, a self-affirmation without an independent basis. Rather, it expresses the fact that our forces are actually faculties. Our pleasure is the pleasure of the practical subject assuring himself of himself.

Kant supports his answer by arguing that the object of the aesthetic-pleasurable relation to the self "can be nothing but the mental state in which we are when imagination and understanding are in free play (insofar as they harmonize with each other as required for *cognition in general*)," for this "subjective relation" of harmony is "suitable for a cognition in general" (*CJ*, §9, B29; 62). Only in reciprocal harmony do our two cognitive forces, imagination and understanding, form the cognitive faculty. The imagination and the understanding each has its own categorically different mode of operation, and the conjunction of these two modes is the condition of the possibility of cognition. The two forces must therefore be *capable* of conjunction. This capability is the "subjective condition" of cognition, and we experience that the condition is met, that our forces are mutually suited, in the "reciprocal harmony" between them in their aesthetic enlivenment. Aesthetic pleasure, according to Kant, is rooted in the experience that the two forces are in harmony.

The basis of the aesthetic judgment of taste, as Kant summarizes this central idea of his aesthetics in the "deduction of pure aesthetic judgments,"

---

* "**Proposition 53.** When the mind regards its own self and its power of activity, it feels pleasure, and the more so the more distinctly it imagines itself and its power of activity."

For "**Proposition 54.** . . . **Proof.** The mind's conatus, or power, is the very essence of the mind. . . . But the essence of the mind affirms only what the mind is and can do (as is self-evident), and not what the mind is not and cannot do. So the mind endeavors to think only of what affirms, or posits, its power of activity."

Hence also "**Proposition 55.** When the mind thinks of its own impotence, by that very fact it feels pain" (Spinoza, *Ethics* [chap. 1, n. 10], part III, 306).

is only the subjective formal condition of a judgment as such. The subjective condition of all judgments is our very ability to judge, i.e., the
power of judgment. When we use this power of judgment in regard to
a presentation by which an object is given, then it requires that there be
a harmony between two presentational powers, imagination (for the
intuition and the combination of its manifold) and understanding (for
the concept that is the presentation of the unity of this combination).
Now since a judgment of taste is not based on a concept of the object
(in the case of a presentation by which an object is given), it can consist
only in the subsumption of the very imagination under the condition
for the understanding to proceed in general from intuition to concepts.
In other words, since the imagination's freedom consists precisely in its
schematizing without a concept, a judgment of taste must rest upon a
mere sensation, namely, our sensation of both the imagination in its
freedom and the understanding with its *lawfulness*, as they reciprocally
enliven each other; i.e., it must rest on a feeling that allows us to judge
the object by the purposefulness that the presentation (by which an
object is given) has insofar as it furthers the cognitive powers in their
free play. (*CJ*, §35, B145–46; 151; translation modified)

Aesthetic pleasure flows from the experience that we are capable of
cognition—that we are capable of capability, that we have practical
faculties. According to Kant, the aesthetic enlivenment of the forces
interrupts the exercise of praxis only in order to let the subject experience that he has the faculty necessary for the exercise of praxis. The
state of the cognitive forces in nondeterminative aesthetic reflection is
evidence of their suitability to their determinative employment in
cognition.

This argument is based on one decisive presupposition hidden in the
transition from the "enlivenment" of the cognitive forces to their "reciprocal harmony." To Kant, the two terms seem to designate the same
thing. Aesthetic pleasure is the "sensation of [an] effect: the facilitated
play of the two mental powers (imagination and understanding) enlivened by their reciprocal harmony" (*CJ*, §9, B31; 63; translation modified). Yet Kant offers no argument to support the claim that the
enlivenment of the cognitive forces must necessarily entail their reciprocal harmony. Indeed, there is no argument. On the contrary, if we follow the aesthetic of the obscure, on which Kant draws in his critique of
Baumgarten, the enlivenment of a force consists in its heightened or

accelerated "motion," which obeys no rule and, hence, cannot be in agreement or harmony with the motion of another force. For forces to be in agreement or harmony, they must be determined. The aesthetic enlivenment or heightening of forces, however, consists precisely in their exceeding any one determination.[1]

This shows that a contradiction lies hidden in Kant's explanation of aesthetic pleasure. By describing aesthetic reflection as an "enlivening" of the forces of representation, Kant turns, with the aesthetics of the obscure, against Baumgarten's conception of the aesthetic as another form of clear cognition. Yet by subsequently describing the aesthetic enlivenment as an experience of the "reciprocal harmony" of the cognitive forces, he retracts the theory of the aesthetic "motion" as a play of obscure force. Instead, he subjects this "motion" to the logic of faculties and their practices. Kant wants to have his cake and eat it, too. On the one hand, he describes the aesthetic as the other of the praxis of determining. In doing so, he draws on the aesthetics of the obscure: the aesthetic is an "enlivening" of the forces that exceeds any practical faculty. On the other hand, the aesthetic must not contradict the logic of faculties, of praxis, of the subject. The aesthetic unleashing of the play of forces must not let us experience anything except the fact that these forces are, in their essence, practical faculties. Kant wants the aesthetic to be an interruption of praxis that does not amount to a rupture in praxis.

From Kant's perspective, aesthetic experience and philosophical insight are two modes of self-reflection that correspond to one another. They differ in their medium—the aesthetic mode of reflection is sensitive; the philosophical is cognitive—yet they do not differ in their substance. In aesthetic reflection, we learn through sensation that we are capable of cognition, for it is precisely in their enlivened and free play that our forces show us that they are faculties through which we can perform the practices of determining.

Yet these same practical faculties also constitute the object of philosophical insight. Philosophy is about the conditions of the possibility of successful practices. For Kant, what we learn in the sensation of aesthetic pleasure is the same as what we understand in philosophical insight:[2] that we possess the faculty of cognition (because imagination and understanding are *of themselves* in harmony) and that we are subjects. Yet if Kant's double description of the aesthetic state of the cognitive forces—in terms of both their "enlivening" *and* their "reciprocal harmony—seems contradictory, then the unity of aesthetic self-experience and philosophical self-cognition at which his argument aims is similarly problematic. And so commences—recommences—the contention between the two.

THE OLD AND THE NEW CONTENTION

In the *Politeia*, Plato speaks of a "contention [*diaphora*] between philosophy and poetry" revolving around the claim to knowledge (607b). And already Plato calls this contention an "ancient" one. Before and long after Plato, philosophy and poetry contended for the title of wisdom—of the knowledge of the good.[3] Each side claimed that it alone possessed practical knowledge in its highest form, the one that was conducive to the good life. And each side contended that the other was incapable of substantiating its claim. Philosophy contended that poetry knows nothing at all; poetry contended that what philosophy knows has no practical use. As Xenophanes writes, "from the beginning all have learned according to Homer," yet "not from the beginning did gods intimate all things to mortals, but as they search in time they discover better."[4] Thus poetry cannot know anything, for it does not search [*suchen*] or examine [*untersuchen*]. In its defense, poetry claimed that the philosophical search for knowledge is laughable, if not even dangerous. Philosophy cannot achieve knowledge that can guide our actions; thus the philosopher is a comic or tragic figure.[5]

This ancient debate will come to an end only when both sides, exhausted by the endless thrust and parry, begin to conceive of themselves in different terms—when both art and philosophy stop claiming that they and they alone can ensure the success of praxis and, instead, start seeing themselves as forms of reflection on praxis. Such a possibility begins to emerge in Baumgarten's definition of the liberal arts and of beautiful thinking as a perfect form of sensibility: the perfect form shows us what sensibility essentially is. In Baumgarten, reflection thus remains tied to perfection, to the goal of aesthetic improvement. In the Kantian sense, in contrast, the aesthetic shows what the ordinary is—without any claim to its perfection. The aesthetic is not a model of an improvement of praxis but a medium of reflection on it.

The same holds for philosophy, which, now mindful that it is ridiculous or even dangerous, concedes its claim to wisdom and becomes reflective. Philosophy no longer conceives of itself as the only or the highest form of knowledge of the good but, instead, as knowledge of the form of the good. This is not to say that philosophy abandons the subject of the good, of the success of praxis; it explores the issue in a different way. No longer is the question, what does the success of praxis consist in—let alone, what *should* it consist in. Instead the question is how (as in how is it possible) to conceive that such success has in fact come to pass. Philosophy asks how we must understand that we gain true understanding, that we offer compelling arguments, that we pass just judgments, that we do good deeds—or, more precisely, that we *can* do these things. Philosophy inquires into the conditions of the possibility of practical success, examining the faculties that render us subjects and thus competent participants in praxis. Philosophical reflection becomes the self-reflection of the subject—on his cognition *as* a subject and on the faculties that enable his successes.

The question arises how the two modes of reflection on praxis will relate once philosophy and the arts concede their claim to wisdom and are thereby transformed. Kant has a two-part answer based on the concept that philosophy and art differ in their media but are identical in substance. Philosophical reflection examines the correspondence between faculties and success, which defines the concept of praxis. In addition, aesthetic experience shows the "subjective condition" of this adequacy, the free harmony of the forces that cooperate as faculties in practical performances.

This double answer, which links the philosophical and aesthetic modes of reflection, falls apart because Kant cannot prove the claim of "harmony" on the description of the aesthetic "enlivenment" of forces—the basis of the phenomenological foundations of his aesthetics—which he adopts from the anti-Baumgartian aesthetics of obscurity. That is why we must conceive of the reflectivity of the aesthetic, as well as the relationship between the aesthetic and the philosophical forms of reflection, in a different way from Kant. Once we do that, it becomes evident that the philosophical and the aesthetic modes of reflection differ not only in their form but also in the images of praxis they delineate. Yet because these are images of *one and the same* praxis, another conflict arises between them.

This "new contention," now between philosophy and the aesthetic, is a contention between agreement and antagonism: it is a contention over whether praxis is ruled, in its heart, by agreement or by antagonism. Philosophical reflection, which inquires into the conditions of the possibility of success and answers this question with the concept of the faculty, is thus a thinking about agreement—about the agreement of faculties and success, ability and the good—for the exercise of a faculty *consists* in the successful realization of a praxis. Philosophical reflection, then, does not "discover" an agreement between faculties and success (or between my faculties and yours, or, ultimately, between my faculties and yours and ours)—as though this agreement were empirically the case and might also not be the case. Philosophy demonstrates that this agreement is something we presuppose when we conceive of ourselves as subjects and of our actions as a praxis.

The aesthetic experience of the play of forces, by contrast, arouses in us a "feeling of indissoluble antagonism between the absolute and the relative."[6] This concerns the relationship between the enlivened force and its expression in aesthetic play. Forces exist only in operation, in engendering an expression. Yet the operation of forces, conceived of as an "obscure" operation, is always the generation of an expression from the one that preceded it. To engender an expression means, in the aesthetic play, to transcend an expression. In their operation, then, forces always enter into an antagonism with the expression they engender. The aesthetic forces are, to use Schlegel's term, "absolute," because they are fundamentally excessive. That is what we experience in the aesthetic play. Yet we also experience the aesthetic play of force as emerging in a process of aestheticization, of a regressive-reflective transformation of the faculties, from the praxis of the subject, and so the aesthetic "feeling" of antagonism extends to this praxis as well. We experience aesthetically that an antagonism lies concealed in the praxis of the subject that is released and, indeed, unleashed in the aestheticization of this praxis, in the unfolding of the play of forces. That is how praxis appears to us in the aesthetic: as already containing within itself the antagonism between force and expression.

Three propositions can serve to summarize this "new" contention between philosophy and the aesthetic:

(1) Philosophical reflection delineates an image of praxis in which faculties and successes correspond. The aesthetic discloses the antagonism of force and expression in praxis.

(2) Philosophy examines faculties as the basis of success. The aesthetic experiences forces as the groundlessness of their expression.

(3) Philosophy unfolds the rationality of praxis, for reason is the totality of the faculties that guarantee success. The aesthetic unleashes the intoxication of forces, for intoxication is the state of the free operation of forces.

With regard to their substantial positions as modes of reflection on praxis, philosophy and the aesthetic are opponents. Yet if the conflict between them cannot be decided, might it be possible to avoid it? For what each posits in opposition to the other—the agreement between faculties and success and the antagonism between force and expression—concerns one and the same praxis. However, it concerns it only in the respective perspective of philosophical consideration *or* aesthetic experience. Only when aesthetic experience enters into philosophical consideration, when philosophical consideration refers to aesthetic experience, does the latent opposition between them erupt into the open.

That is what happens in aesthetics, and this marks another difference between the old contention between philosophy and poetry and the new one between philosophical and aesthetic reflection. The first difference concerns the two parties to the disagreement—between whom does it take place? The second difference concerns the site of this disagreement—where does it takes place? The old contention between philosophy and poetry mentioned by Plato concerns philosophy at its core—in its conception of itself. Yet this should not define philosophy: the contention with poetry should help philosophy gain its self-conception and self-confidence, but then—this is the hope Plato expressed in the image of the expulsion of the poets—the dispute should come to an end.

With aesthetics, by contrast, the relation of philosophy to the aesthetic moves to the very core of philosophy. This change has been described (by Baumgarten: *Aesthetics*, §6; see p. 45) as meaning that the aesthetic becomes an object "worthy" of philosophy. Yet the aesthetic cannot be a mere *object* of philosophy. It is a mode of reflection on praxis that runs counter to the philosophical mode. So when philosophy turns, as aesthetics, to the aesthetic, it draws on a mode of reflection on praxis that is antagonistic to its own—the philosophical—mode of reflection. The aesthetic, as an object of philosophy, is also its opponent. Aesthetics thus carries the contention between the philosophical and the aesthetic modes of reflections into philosophy.

Aesthetics is the philosophy of the aesthetic. As the philosophy *of the aesthetic*, aesthetics turns to the aesthetic reflection on praxis and reconstructs how practical faculties are transformed by their aestheticization into obscure forces. Yet aesthetics does this *as philosophy*—not merely as aesthetic experience or aesthetic criticism. Aesthetics does not merely point up aesthetic events; it is the thinking of aesthetic events. Yet aesthetic events cannot be thought of in the same way philosophy thinks of practical performances. Practical faculties are not transformed into obscure forces by the exercise of a practical faculty: the process of aestheticization is not a praxis. So philosophy cannot inquire into faculties that guarantee success. By becoming aesthetics and turning to the aesthetic, philosophy turns to something that calls into question the form of philosophical thinking itself. With aesthetics, the *concept* of philosophy changes. We can designate this change (drawing on Herder and anticipating Nietzsche) by saying that with aesthetics—that is to say, with the attempt not merely to experience or to critically point up the aesthetic event but to think it—philosophy becomes *genealogy*.

The process of aestheticization consists in the transformation of practical faculties into forces at obscure play. In this transformation, aestheticization—that is why the aesthetic is also a "mode of reflection"—shows us the practical faculties in a different way, in the transition into forces at obscure play. This transition of faculties into forces is experienced in the aesthetic; the challenge to understand it is what turns philosophy into genealogy. For the central claim of genealogy is this: practical faculties are always in transition into forces at obscure play because they are always still emerging from obscure forces. Obscure forces are the other of practical faculties *only* because they are the ground from which the practical faculties emerge. Obscure forces make practical faculties possible.

The philosophy that, in thinking aestheticization, becomes genealogy describes faculties as the point where two dimensions of enablement intersect: the enablement of success by practical faculties and the enablement of these practical faculties themselves by obscure forces. Faculties are the *condition of the possibility of practical success*, and forces are the *condition of the possibility of practical faculties*. Yet the terms "possibility" and "condition" mean different things in both contexts.

The faculty guarantees practical success; the exercise of the faculty *is* the successful performance of a praxis. The force, by contrast, has a margin of play over and against the laws of mechanics and the purposes of life, a margin that renders the formation of faculties in practice at once possible and impossible.[7] The essential indeterminacy of the play of obscure forces frees man from the reign of mechanical laws, as well as biological purposes, enabling him to become, as the "sense of an alien . . . imprints itself within [him]," a subject of faculties. Yet the essential indeterminacy of forces at obscure play also makes it impossible to identify "man" with "subject." The emergence of the practical faculties from their other, from obscure forces, remains inscribed on them. In other words, inscribed on the faculty is its other—the obscure force from which and against which it emerges. That is why the genealogical insight into the emergence of the faculty from the obscure force—the insight that what enables the faculty also makes it impossible—immediately changes the philosophical conception of how faculties are exercised, what a praxis is, and what accounts for its success.

Thinking of the aesthetic event within a genealogical philosophy changes the concept of praxis. Since the force from which and against which the faculty emerges remains inscribed on it, there are no faculties in the pure sense and no performance whose logic and energy can be conceived in its entirety by the formal definitions. The very use of the concepts of "faculty," "praxis," and "subject" entails the opposing concepts of "force," "play," and "man." What we call "faculty," "praxis," "subject" is forever compromised by the very fact that it internally divides into faculty *and* force, praxis *and* play, subject *and* man.

The philosophical thinking of the aesthetic event leads to a genealogical understanding of practical faculties and thus delineates a program of philosophical inquiries. This program demands that we seek out in all domains of human praxis the division of faculty against itself, its being split into faculty and force, always asking which particular form this division takes.[8]

CHAPTER SIX

Ethics: The Freedom of Self-Creation

WHAT CONSTITUTES THE "ethical-political import" of the aesthetic?[1] How does one solve "the problem" of finding the culture that is "appropriate to our music"[2] and that would fit our aesthetic praxis and theory of art? In other words, how must a culture be constituted to be an aesthetic culture? To think of the aesthetic philosophically, Nietzsche writes, means to raise these questions and deal with the problems they present. For the aesthetic way of doing and contemplating art are not limited to the domain of art. The aesthetic cannot, and should not, concern art alone. The aesthetic praxis and theory of art change "culture"—both the "ethical" way the individual conducts his or her life and the "political" way the community conducts its affairs.

"Nietzsche's meditation on art," as Heidegger rightly noted—misunderstanding, however, the implications of his own observations—"keeps to the traditional path. The path is defined in its peculiarity by the term 'aesthetics'" (*Nietzsche*, IV, 77). Nietzsche's theory of art, which he first develops in *The Birth of Tragedy* and whose fundamental features he will keep unchanged despite the later self-criticism, is not his own invention, the intentionally unfamiliar terminology notwithstanding. It is a reformulation, a recovery of insights first framed in the fragmentary approaches to an aesthetics of the obscure between Baumgarten and Kant. Nietzsche's early essay is of incomparable importance—not because he is saying something for the first time, but because he reframes the original insight of the aesthetics of the obscure *against* the attempts to appropriate this insight for the programs of self-assurance in the philosophies of German idealism, beginning with Kant. By stressing its true meaning, Nietzsche recovers the aesthetics of the obscure not merely as a theory of the beautiful or of the arts but also as a description of the human being, which is of ethical-political and cultural import. That is why "the problem of finding the culture that is appropriate to our music" marks the beginning and end of Nietzsche's philosophy. And it is why Nietzsche begins and ends his philosophy with one and the same double move: he emphasizes the categorical difference separating the aesthetic from the cognitive and moral practices, and he simultaneously recognizes the decisive power of the aesthetic to change these practices.

LEARNING FROM THE ARTISTS

The power to change our practices, our life, according to Nietzsche in *The Gay Science*, earns art *"our ultimate gratitude."* Without art, things "would be utterly unbearable" (*GS*, 107; 104). Later, in his preface to the second edition, Nietzsche explains what sort of art he is thinking of: not "that whole romantic uproar and tumult of the senses that is loved by the educated mob, together with its aspirations towards the sublime, the elevated, the distorted." Rather, it is *"another kind* of art—a mocking, light, fleeting, divinely untroubled, divinely artificial art that, like a bright flame, blazes into an unclouded sky!" (*GS*, preface to the second edition; 7–8) This "other kind of art," which is of ethical-political import, is an art made and imagined in a different way: "Above all [it is] an art for artists, only for artists!"

Distancing himself in this way from the romantic art of sensual excitation, Nietzsche adopts once more the position of aesthetic autonomy from *The Birth of Tragedy*.* The "art for artists" is opposed to a "rhetorical" art, which—like Euripides's aesthetic Socratism or Wagner's culture-industrial *Gesamtkunstwerk*—is calculated to produce effects in the spectators.[3] An "art for artists" is not made for the spectators: it follows its own laws. Yet Nietzsche's "an art for artists, only for artists!" is not a mere repetition of the program of aesthetic autonomy. It adds the essential insight that aesthetically autonomous art gains ethical-political im-

---

* "Anyone seeking to derive the effect of the tragic from these moral sources alone, however, as was the normal practice in aesthetics for far too long, should not believe that this does anything to benefit art, since the first demand of art must be for purity in its own realm" (*BT*, 24; 113).

port only through the figure of the artist—more precisely, through our *learning from the artists.*

Under the heading "What one should learn from artists," section 299 of *The Gay Science*, Nietzsche challenges us to explore the actions and abilities of artists:

> All this we should learn from artists while otherwise being wiser than they. For usually in their case this delicate power stops where art ends and life begins; *we*, however, want to be poets of our lives, starting with the smallest and most commonplace details. (*GS*, 299; 170)

The artist moves to the center because he *does something*; that is, he has an ability. To learn from the artists means to take up doing *in the way* of the artists—only "more wisely"—by using the "power" learned from the artists to answer a different question: the question of the wise, the philosophical question, the question regarding the good life.

TO BE ABLE TO BE UNABLE

What do artists do—or, more important, *how* do they do what they do? In *The Gay Science*, where Nietzsche makes a first attempt to describe a program of learning from the artists, he defines artists as "worshippers of shapes, tones, words." Their ability, which we are to learn from them and bring to bear on our own lives, is described as follows: "to stop bravely at the surface, the fold, the skin; to worship semblance, to believe in shapes, tones, words—in the whole Olympus of semblance" (*GS*, preface to the second edition; 8–9; translation modified). The ability of artists consists in persevering in semblance; in other words, it consists in an inability. Artists are "good at *not* knowing" (ibid., 8), good at persisting in mere semblance—indeed, embracing semblance—in the quest for knowledge.

The Gay Science limits the ability of artists to this activity of not knowing. Here aesthetics becomes, quite literally, a phenomenology. Art embodies "the *good* will to semblance," and through art we achieve—as *The Gay Science* puts it in a half-ironic quotation of the well-known passage from *The Birth of Tragedy*—a vision even of ourselves as an "aesthetic phenomenon." "As an aesthetic phenomenon existence is still *bearable* to us, and art furnishes us with the eye and hand and, above all, the good conscience to be *able* to make such a phenomenon out of ourselves" (*GS* 107; 104). The ability one learns from artists is an ability to *see*, to see oneself *in a different way*, as mere semblance, as an aesthetic phenomenon. Those who have learned to do this gain a "*freedom over things*," which is due to the distance aesthetic contemplation maintains even from itself. "At times we need to have a rest from ourselves by looking at and down at ourselves and, from an artistic distance, laughing *at* ourselves or crying *at* ourselves" (*GS* 107; 104). Someone who looks at himself in this way can also act differently: he can "float and play" (*GS* 107; 105).

What this aesthetic phenomenology, this doctrine of semblance ignores is nothing less than the central insight in *The Birth of Tragedy*: that the aesthetic semblance originates in a condition that contradicts it. Aesthetic semblance is semblance experienced as semblance—"semblance reduced [*depotenzirt*] to semblance"[4]—because it is experienced as an engendered semblance. Furthermore, drawing on the insight from *The Birth of Tragedy*, aesthetic semblance is engendered by something that is not itself this semblance but its antagonist: the "complete unchaining of all symbolic forces" in intoxication (*BT*, 2; 21; translation modified). Aesthetic semblance is the paradoxical effect of intoxication. It is engendered in intoxication and against it by a "redemption" and an absolution from intoxication (*BT*, 4; 25–26).

Yet if art is not merely the "*good* will to semblance" because it lets us experience, with the semblance, the intoxicated unchaining of the force to engender and to dissolve it, then we cannot, as *The Gay Science* does, also conceive of the ability of the artists to transform reality into an aesthetic phenomenon. That is why Nietzsche, in *Twilight of the Idols*, returns once more—but now with a different perspective, the perspective of a "psychology of the artist"—to his concept of intoxication: "For there to be art, for there to be any kind of aesthetic doing and seeing, one physiological precondition is indispensable: *intoxication*" (*RRUM*, 8; 46–47).

In intoxication, things change: "Man in this state transforms things" (*RRUM*, 9; 47). Intoxication is a way of doing that transforms things "into perfection." "This *need* to transform into perfection is—art" (ibid.). According to the traditional theory of artistic making, conceived as "poetics," a thing's perfect shape is implicit in it; the artistic doing brings it to the fore. Artistic doing is understood as a form of production, a purposeful work of engendering. "Purposeful" means that, for the doer, the performance of the doing is the reason—the purpose—for his doing. He does in order to realize his purpose. He therefore knows what it is he is doing, and the realization of his purpose is the consequence of, the reason for, his doing. By contrast, in the act of artistic perfection conceived as an intoxicated doing, the doer's purpose is not realized by a doing or an activity that he knows and wills. What the intoxicated agent realizes is—himself: "Man in this state transforms things until they reflect his power—until they are reflections of his perfection" (ibid.). The "aesthetic doing and seeing" thus *entail* a transformation of things, a bringing-to-perfection. But this transformation is not what the artistic doing *performs*: performance is not the purpose of this doing. There is no purpose to the artistic doing that would ground and direct it. The artistic doing is the "reflection" or "communication" (*RRUM*, 10; 48) of the state in which the artist is as he does.

This inversion—the artistic doing is the self-"communication" of the doer rather than the realization of a purpose—corresponds to the state of the subject in the artistic doing. When Nietzsche describes this state as an "intoxication," he means, as in *The Birth of Tragedy*, a state of "increased force and plenitude" (*RRUM*, 8; 47; translation modified), a state he once again calls "Dionysian":

> In the Dionysian state . . . the whole system of the emotions is aroused and intensified so that it discharges its every means of expression at one stroke, at the same time forcing out the power to represent, reproduce, transfigure, transform, every kind of mime and play-acting. (*RRUM*, 10; 48; translation modified)

When we understand the purposeful actions of a subject as displays of his capacities, we conceive of these actions as particular realizations of a universal form of which the agent is aware (and hence capable of orienting and correcting himself). Faculties of action are essentially conscious. By contrast, Nietzsche's term *Kräfte*—forces—refers to an effective doing beyond (or short of) consciousness; forces are unconscious. That is precisely what the concept of intoxication means. Intoxication is a state in which the forces of the subject are heightened so as to escape his conscious control. Or, conversely, the unchaining of forces in intoxication consists in their exceeding the aggregate state of self-conscious faculties in purposeful action. That is why intoxicated man, man in the state of heightened forces, is defined by an essential inability—"the inability *not* to react (as with certain hysterics who also enter into any role at the slightest sign)" (ibid.). It is also an incapacity to be able to act, *as* the force of the aesthetic needs to react, in order to express himself.

In *Twilight of the Idols*, Nietzsche calls intoxication the "physiological precondition" of "aesthetic doing and seeing." Intoxication, then, is not the whole of the artistic doing. The artist is not entirely (and not always) intoxicated, and his relationship with intoxication is ambivalent. The artist *plays with* intoxication: the world of art "reveals itself in a playing with intoxication, not in complete entrapment by it. In the actor we recognize Dionysian man, the instinctive poet, singer, dancer, but Dionysian man as he is *played*."[5] This distinguishes the Dionysian artist from the "Dionysian Barbarians" (*BT*, 2; 20). Their barbarism is a state of simple lack of ability and consists in a "regress[ion] to the condition of tigers and monkeys." The Dionysian artist, by contrast, is divided; he is marked by a "strange mixture and duality in [his] affects" (ibid., 21). The artist is self-conscious faculty *and* force unchained in intoxication. Even more, he is the transition from one to the other and back again. The artist has a peculiar ability: the ability of inability. The artist is able to be unable.[6]

IF THE ARTIST'S ABILITY is an ability of inability, then to learn from the artists means to unlearn: to "learn ... to forget well" (*GS*, preface to the second edition; 8)—to learn the ability to forget one's ability and what one is able to do. *The Gay Science* challenges us to learn the artists' "delicate power," their paradoxical ability to exceed or fall short of their practical faculties. The reason that the ethical-political import of aesthetic art turns on the artist is that the artist is the model of a way of doing that is different—*different* from purposeful action. Nonetheless, learning from the artist does not mean escaping from participation in the world of praxis into the aesthetic contemplation of semblance. Drawing on the model of the artist for orientation does not mean replacing the things of praxis with "aesthetic phenomena" but, rather, with an aesthetic transformation of the world of praxis.

This program of an aestheticization of praxis aims at a way of performing doing—a way that is different from the model of action. "Aestheticization of praxis" means to break the dominion of the concept of action (as well as all of the concepts it entails, such as purpose, reasons, intention, faculty, self-consciousness, and so on) over one's doing. The artist teaches that one can do in a way *different* from the purposeful and self-conscious exercise of practical faculties. The term Nietzsche uses to designate this other way of doing, falling short of or exceeding in terms of action, is *Leben* (life). To take up doing according to the model of artists means not to act but to "live."

The fundamental move of an aestheticization of praxis, then, consists in learning from the model of the artist to make a conceptual distinction between action and life in terms of doing. The first result of this newly acquired skill is a redescription of the field of praxis. One who has learned from the artists that there is a doing beyond action discerns how the practical everywhere—at its lower, as well as its upper, margins—unravels into the living. At both its lower and its upper margins, the practical calls for a terminology that avoids action. "Life," according to this aesthetic redescription, is both the most basic (descriptively, the most elementary) and the supreme (normatively, the most exacting) concept in a philosophy of praxis: "life" defines *movement* and the *good*.

LIVING MOVEMENT

A thinking that conceives of doing in accordance with the concept of action is a thinking seduced by morality.[7] To speak of actions means to attribute processes to a subject such that these processes appear as logical consequences of the subject's attitudes, which, taken together, form the reason for these processes. The concept of action thus enables one to speak of a subject as the "author" of these processes and to hold him responsible for them. "The most ancient and long-established psychology was at work here . . . in its eyes every event was an action, every action the result of a will; in its eyes the world became a multiplicity of agents, an agent (a 'subject') foisting himself onto every event" (*TI*, "The Four Great Errors," 3; 28).[8] This is why the concept of action was invented: so that instead of complaining about mere events and their consequences, we can complain about *a person*, the "subject" of the action, who is to blame for them. Because someone performed the action for a reason, he can be criticized for performing one action *instead* of another; using Nietzsche's example: for devouring as a bird of prey the little lambs instead of sparing them.

Nietzsche offered different versions of his critique of the concept of action. In one version, he claims that there is no subject who could decide between alternatives because every decision, just as every act, is an expression of the subject's own being. In other words, there is no freedom because everything is determined. In a second version, Nietzsche maintains that we cannot attribute an action to a subject *as his own doing* because there is no logical connection between the subject's "inner" states and his "exterior" action. In other words, because everything is causal, there is no intentionality. These two versions of Nietzsche's critique of the concept of action ultimately dispute the notion that there is a difference between purposeful action and a causally determined event.[9] In a third version, however, his critique aims to undermine the completeness and hence the validity of the alternative between teleology and causality. In this version, Nietzsche does not deny that we can attribute a doing, as opposed to an event, to a subject as *that subject's* doing. Yet he disputes the notion that this attribution requires us to understand that the doing was performed because of the subject's reasons, as a realization of his purposes and hence as his action. Human doing cannot be identified with purposeful action.[10]

Nietzsche initially tries to define the difference between doing and action (which he will shortly thereafter develop into the concept of the "will to power") in unpublished fragments that he describes as *"attempts at an extra-moral consideration of the world"* (*Fragments, 1880*, 31). If such "attempts" are not to be taken "too lightly," then the extramoral consideration of the world is an aesthetic one ("the worship of genius")* that sees the world *"through the prism of the artist"* (*BT*, "An Attempt at Self-Criticism"; 5). Nietzsche uses a contemptuous simile to describe "the

* *"Attempts at an extra-moral consideration of the world*: previously attempted by me too lightly—an *aesthetic* consideration (the worship of genius—)" (*Fragments, 1880*, 1[120]; 31).

genius," who is "like a blind sea-crab, continually groping in all directions and *occasionally* catching something; yet it does not grope in order to catch but because its limbs need the exercise" (*Fragments, 1880*, 1[53]; 17).

The aesthetic genius offers the spectacle of a peculiar way of doing. The first defining feature of this doing is that it is "blind." It is not directed by a perception that would provide the doer with knowledge of what objects are before him so that he can "catch" them. This description still presupposes what the second and more profound defining feature calls into question: that this "groping" is a doing that seeks to catch—to snatch and obtain—something. However, the aesthetic doing is not performed for the sake of something, not even—the alternative offered by Aristotle—for its own sake. The genius performs it the way the sea crab moves: "because its limbs need the exercise." Like an action, then, the aesthetic doing is *someone's* doing. But in contrast to action, in aesthetic doing the subject gives free exercise to his forces unfettered by all purpose rather than realizing his purposes by means of his faculties.

This is not the case merely with the doings of the sea crab and the genius but in human doing in general. "Very few *actions* occur for purposes; most of them are mere *doings*—movements in which a force is discharged" (ibid., 1[127]; 33). These groping attempts at an "extra-moral" consideration of doing lead to a specific concept—the concept of life: "all that lives, moves; this doing does not exist for specific purposes, it is life itself" (ibid., 1[70]; 21). To the extent that human doing is living movement, it is not reducible to the model of purposeful action. For "life," as Nietzsche sees it, does not designate a teleology without self-consciousness, as in the Aristotelian tradition. Rather, it designates an expression without purpose:* the "purposeless *overflowing* of force" (ibid., 1[44]; 15).

---

* "Physiologists should think twice before positioning the drive for self-preservation as the cardinal drive of an organic being. Above all, a living thing wants to *discharge* its strength—life itself is will to power—: self-preservation is only one of the indirect and most frequent *consequences* of this.—In short, here as elsewhere, watch out for *superfluous* teleological principles!" (*BGE*, 13; 15).

A DIFFERENT GOOD

The vitality of human doing, discerned in the aesthetic perspective, defies the model of purposeful action: human doing, as living doing, is not the realization of a purpose but the expression of a force. Yet, although Nietzsche sometimes seems to say as much, living movement and purposeful action are not two different, let alone separate, types of human doing. On the contrary, despite and, in fact, because of their constitutional antagonism, living movement is a precondition of the success of purposeful action.

This is certainly the case if the ability to innovate, to invent, is an essential feature of the successful performance of actions. We say that we *make* an invention or innovation in the sense that we bring about something that has not existed before. However, we can change something only by exposing ourselves to a change. This is indicated by the concept of experiment or "test," in which we combine active intervention on our part—the establishment of experimental conditions—with a willingness to expose ourselves to events that take their own course. Thus, making an invention or an innovation is not entirely a purposeful act. It requires an openness toward the accidental:

> An *accidental* concurrence of two words or of a word and a spectacle is the origin of a new thought. (*Fragments, 1880*, 1[51]; 17)

The concept of accident marks the moment at which the doing breaks loose from action, transcends its purpose; the moment at which the subject does something more (or less or different) than he wanted and perhaps more than he can; the moment at which his forces "exercise" themselves and their vitality, at which his doing comes "alive." "Actions whose successful outcome is *unexpected*, actions undertaken for a *different purpose*—, an animal that guards its eggs as *nourishment* and suddenly sees beings of its own kind" (ibid., 1[54]; 17). From the perspective of the old, all innovation occurs suddenly, accidentally. It does not happen as a consequence of reasons, as a realization of purposes I already have, but because my forces are alive in an unknown situation, before an unknown object.

And this holds true not only in the case of the "unexpected successful outcome," the invention of an entirely different purpose and an entirely different possible action. It holds true for all truly successful actions—even ones that I have long been able to perform. The analogy of purposeful action defines practical success as follows: practical success is purpose corresponding to action as cause corresponds to effect. I exercise my practical faculty and thus bring my action to success if I do precisely (and nothing but) what I want to do or what my best reasons tell me to do. By contrast, from the aesthetic perspective, in a contemplation of human doing "under the prism of the artist," the moment of innovation in *all* practical success comes to the fore—even in the most quotidian and ordinary doings. All success bears the mark of a transgression, however small, beyond the intended—and hence familiar—purpose, a transcendence that approximates it to the "unexpected successful outcome." To put it another way, success is not merely ability but also a chance occurrence:[11] the "propitious" accident (*Fragments, 1880,* 1[63]; 19) of a living act exceeding or falling short of purposeful action.

The insight into the difference between action and life reveals the difference *within* action, its *internal* division into ability and accident without which no action succeeds—thus the action-theoretical conclusion Nietzsche draws from the concept of living movement gained in aesthetics. This conclusion is aimed against the moral concept of action and is drawn from an "extra-moral" consideration. A moral consideration is concerned with responsibility and presupposes that what a subject does can be understood as a realization of the purpose he pursues. The moral game of judgment—reproach, accountability, punishment—is based on the model of action, of a correspondence between doing and purpose. Yet if a living movement operates in all action, especially where it succeeds, and if a living movement—although its performance occurs in a self, as an expression of its forces—is not performed by a subject as the execution of an action, then the vitality of movement opens a door through which a moment of unaccountability enters into all action. *This* is why morality "condemns" life (*TI*, "Morality as Anti-Nature," 6; 24): because action eludes the opposite poles of moral valuation, good and evil, by virtue of the momentum of vitality within it.

From the perspective of morality, this elusion is the original evil—not the evil that turns against the good, but the evil that turns against the difference between good and evil. That is why morality must combat vitality and become the "*obstacle* to inventions" (*Fragments, 1880,* 1[43];

15). From the practical perspective, however, morality itself is bad: "*only* ethical: and mankind sinks into poverty, nothing is invented" (ibid.); "moral people would let the world wither" (ibid., 1[38]; 14).* The aesthetic perspective raises an objection against the moral good-or-evil in the name of a different good, a good beyond good and evil, namely, the good that resides in vitality. It is in this extramoral concept of the good that the ethical-political import of the aesthetic resides.

AESTHETIC ENJOYMENT OF SELF

A look back at the model of the artist is helpful at this point. In *The Gay Science*, Nietzsche challenges us to learn from the artists their "delicate power" and to bring it to bear on our own lives. This power of the artists consists in their peculiarly paradoxical ability—their ability to be unable. The artists employ this ability to exceed or fall short of their faculties in order to make something out of the intoxicated unchaining of their force. Yet this does not define the state of living forces at its core: "One is active because all that lives must move—*not* **for the sake** of joy, that is, *without purpose*: though there is joy in it" (*Fragments, 1880*, 1[45]; 16). This is a joy taken in the living operation of the forces themselves and, because it is the living operation of one's own forces, a joy or delight taken in oneself. This joy or delight, which is merely implied in everyday life, becomes the defining feature in the intoxicated heightening and unchaining of these forces, which is the "physiological precondition" of "aesthetic seeing and doing." "[I]n art man finds enjoyment in himself as perfection" (*RRUM*, 9; 47). The artists enjoy the intoxicated state of heightened forces, and, since all enjoyment implies valuation, they judge this state itself to be good. In the pleasure they take in their own aesthetic condition, the artists see another good revealed, one that differs from the practical goodness of actively realized purposes.

A heightened form of this phenomenon is manifest in the figure of the tragic artist. His art is "tragic" to the extent that it "reveals much that is ugly, harsh, questionable in life" (*RRUM*, 24; 55). In order to under-

---

* "As useful and unpleasant as a well-oiled *keyhole*" (*Fragments, 1880*, 1[92]; 26) is Nietzsche's simile for action according to the image of morality.

stand the ethical-political import of such art, we must ask, as Nietzsche does, what it communicates about the artist himself. We must appeal to the artists themselves to tell us—following Nietzsche's metaphor of potency—that they are *"able."* But in what does their ability consist?

> *What does the tragic artist communicate about himself?* Is it not precisely the state of *fearlessness* in the face of the fearful and questionable that he shows? This state is itself highly desirable: anyone who knows it honours it with the highest honours. He communicates it, he *must* communicate it, so long as he is an artist, a genius of communication. Bravery and unrestrained feeling in the face of a powerful enemy, or noble hardship, or a problem which makes one shudder with horror—it is this *triumphant* state that the tragic artist selects and glorifies. Faced with tragedy, the warlike element in our souls celebrates its Saturnalia; anyone who is used to suffering, who seeks out suffering, the *heroic* person praises his existence through tragedy—to him alone the tragedian offers a draught of this sweetest cruelty. (*RRUM*, 24; 55–56)

The artist is always able to let his forces exercise themselves freely, to unfold them, even heighten them in intoxication. Always—even in the face of fear, despair, and utter defeat. Therein lies the artist's "triumph," therein consists his "ability." Even "in the face of a powerful enemy, or a problem which makes one shudder with horror," the tragic artist can let his forces unfold even where his faculties are destroyed. He remains alive in failure.

The tragic artist, then, is able to do something that is impossible in action: he can affirm tragic failure. To affirm is to approve of something, to judge it to be "good." Yet tragic failure is the failure of the intended purpose, of the practical good. Tragic failure, then, cannot be good in the practical sense. Where the only good is the practical good, tragic failure can be lamented, perhaps also be borne, but never affirmed. Affirmation is possible only in the context of a different good, and this is precisely the tragic artist's ability: he affirms tragic failure because in it he enjoys his own "perfection—because in, and because of, the failure of the good of action the self attains a state it judges, in reflecting upon itself, to be good.

In the "Reconnaissance Raids of an Untimely Man," the chapter of *Twilight of the Idols* that elaborates the theories of artistic intoxication and the tragic artist, Nietzsche discerns in Goethe the exemplary figure of artistic self-affirmation. "He said yes to all" (*RRUM*, 49; 74)—including all that threatened him, indeed all that led him to fail. And even then Goethe could say yes because he was able to enjoy *himself*, experience the unfolding of his own living forces as a good, even in the failure of the good of action. The artist can say yes to all because he can say yes to himself in the face of all. If Nietzsche expresses this in terms of man's finding "in art . . . enjoyment in himself as perfection," this means that there is, for the artist, a good that is categorically *different* from the practical good of action that destroys itself in tragic failure. The power of the artist consists in breaking free, breaking loose from the dominion of the practical good and committing himself to another good: the good of his own state of heightened forces and their playful-living operation.

CREATING ONESELF

How can one "learn" this power from the artists? How can self-affirmation in the aesthetic enjoyment of self have ethical import? How can liberation from the good of action take place not merely in artistic intoxication but also in "real" life, "starting with the smallest and most commonplace details"? What is a good life?

Nietzsche also describes breaking free from the regimentation provided by the practical good as the program of the "immoralist":

> We who are different, we immoralists . . . have opened our hearts to all kinds of understanding, comprehending, *approving*. We do not readily deny; we seek our honour in being *affirmative*. More and more our eyes have been opened to that economy which still needs and can exploit all that is rejected by the holy madness of the priest, of the priest's *sick* reason; to that economy in the law of life which can gain advantage even from the repulsive species of the miseryguts [*sic*], the priest, the virtuous man—*what* advantage? But we ourselves, we immoralists, are the answer here. (*TI*, "Morality as Anti-Nature," 6; 25)

The immoralists' answer to the question regarding the good, regarding a perfection beyond the practical good, is: "we ourselves are the answer here." The good beyond the practical good is the good of the self or the self as good. Because he was an immoralist, Goethe was able to say yes to all, to tolerate and use even what appears from the perspective of the practical good to be defeatist, transgressive, and failed. Goethe did not find fulfillment in participation in practices or in the pursuit of their good. Instead, he *created himself* (*RRUM*, 49; 74), which is to say, he created his good as opposed to the good of practices.

The immoralist's fundamental move, the move he has learned from the artist, consists in a radical operation of discrimination. He distinguishes his good—the good of his own self—from the practical good. He maintains that there is a good that is not practical, that cannot be adapted to the form of a purpose and be actively realized. This distinction constitutes his *im*moralism, his antagonism against morality. For "morality"—in the sense in which the immoralist asserts his opposition—is not any specific system of ethical evaluations or a set of morals defined one way or another. Rather, the morality of morals—what Nietzsche also calls the "ethicality of ethos (*Sittlichkeit der Sitte*)"[12]—is fundamentally an action- and subject-theoretical model. Central to this model is the idea that there exists an indissoluble connection between the good of the self and the good of practices. Practices are social, and the good, morally conceived, is being good *within* social practices—not merely in the sense of the particular good of any given practice but in the sense of the general good of correct participation in social practices. Thus for Ernst Tugendhat, to be morally good means to be good as a "member of the community, as a social partner or a partner in cooperation."[13] The moral virtues—justice, respect, consideration, and so on—enable the subject to participate in social practices in general. Forming, possessing, and applying these virtues define—from the moral point of view—what it means to be good "as a human being." Yet this definition of the moral good is, in fact, a consequence of the formal definition of the good as a practical purpose. For to choose and realize a purpose means to participate, however remotely, in a social practice. Purposefulness and participation in social practices are two sides of the same coin. They form the morality of morals, the ethicality of ethos.

The immoralist's counterprogram consists in discontinuity—a rupture between the good of the self and the good of social participation; a breaking free from the constraints and, indeed, the perspective of the practical good. "To create oneself" means to engender oneself—one's self—*against* the social being one already is. One's creation of oneself, then, is no *creatio ex nihilo*. We "ought to blow to the winds all presumptuous talk of 'willing' and 'creating'" (*Daybreak*, 552, 223). As "human beings . . . who give themselves laws, who create themselves," we must "become the best students and discoverers of everything lawful and necessary in the world" (*GS*, 335; 189). One already *is*—has always been—a subject, a social participant, when one undertakes to create oneself. To create oneself means to break free from oneself as one already is, to distinguish oneself from oneself as a social participant.[14] Yet if one can act purposefully and hence successfully only as a participant in social practices; if one can do good (in the sense of the "ethicality of ethos") only by being a good participant in social practices; then creating oneself so as to distinguish oneself from oneself as a social participant means also to transcend oneself as an agent, as a practical subject. To create oneself means to unlearn the capacity to act because only in this unlearning does one gain another good—the good of living forces revealed in the enjoyment of self.

This constitutes the lesson the immoralist has learned from the artists. The immoralist creator of himself learns from the artists that to create oneself means to distinguish oneself from oneself—as a participant in social practices—from the good of social practices, the undermining of one's own capacity to act and an orientation toward one's own, asocial good. Moreover, the immoralist creator of himself learns from the artists that his own asocial good consists not in a purposeful action but in a state of vitality short of the teleological order of action. To learn from the artists the power to distinguish oneself from the good of social practices and thus to create oneself means learning to distinguish between action and life. It means learning that the good of life is not the same as the good of action, that the good life is not composed of good actions. Life is good to the extent that it is alive.

———

AT THIS POINT, the lesson we learn from artists is to distinguish between the practical exercise of faculties and the playful operation of force, while at the same time being "wiser" than they are by bringing this distinction to bear on life—making the distinction between two classes of performances, actions and movements; between two concepts of the good, as a social purpose and as a living state; between two concepts of the subject, as a social participant and the self that creates itself in enjoyment. Learning from the artists means to learn that the rift within the self is irreparable. It is not merely in the content but also in the form of the good. It is a rift within the good that cannot be rewoven into a unity of any kind.

Yet the artists do not merely make distinctions, they are also able to join what they keep apart. They hold it together as the two sides of the distinction. This separates the artists from the practical subjects (the artists are able *to be unable*), as well as from the Dionysian Barbarians (the artists are *able* to be unable). For the Dionysian Barbarians, the intoxicated unchaining of forces supplants the practical faculties acquired with much effort; the Barbarians feel these faculties to be a burden and wield them without confidence. For the artists, by contrast, their very faculties are transformed into their most highly developed "symbolic forces" (*BT*, 2; 21) and are unchained in intoxication.[15] That is why the intoxicated unchaining of the artist's forces in turn benefits the practical exercise of his faculties. "Using and *discerning* accident: that is called genius" (*Fragments, 1880*, 1[91]; 26). Not even the artists can perform the living operation of their forces for the sake of the success of their actions, for this living operation cannot be performed at all. The artists are able *to be unable*. But because what the artists transform into living playful forces in intoxicated unchaining are their own practical faculties, their aesthetic intoxication also affects their praxis, their actions. Part of the experience of the artists is that the aesthetic suspension of the practical exercise of faculties in the play of living forces leads to the attainment of the good they strive for.

To learn from the artists, therefore, means not only to learn that faculties and forces and hence action and play, the good of action (as social purpose) and the good of play (as living self) are categorically different from one another. It also means to learn that the good of action and the good of play, although divided by a rift, need one another. On the one hand, the good of the living play of forces exists only in a relation of enjoyment of self of which only a subject of practical faculties is capable. In addition, the intoxication of one's forces is a good only for the individual who experiences it from a certain distance, who, as Nietzsche puts it, "plays" this state. On the other hand, the good of the practical exercise of faculties exists only in attempts and experimentation. Only one who exposes himself to accident, to the living play of forces, can be truly successful in his actions. Either form of the good, then, can exist only for one for whom both exist. Neither form of the good is good by itself. Each form presupposes the other, whose doing—as action or as play—it opposes. By looking to the artists, we learn not only the distinction of the good but also the good of distinction.

———

THE GOOD ENGENDERED by the distinction of the good is freedom, and the distinction between action and play, between faculty and force is liberating. That is why Nietzsche calls Goethe, to his mind the paradigmatic artist who was able to say yes beyond the practical good-and-bad, a "*liberated* spirit" (*RRUM*, 49; 74). Goethe, as Nietzsche portrays him in his last book, solves the problem he raised in his first one: the "problem [of finding] the culture appropriate to our music!" Already in the notes for *The Birth of Tragedy*, Nietzsche had inscribed above his "considerations on the ethical-political import of musical drama" the title "tragedy and the free spirits [*Freigeister*]."* But only *Twilight of the Idols* will contain the writing to match this title. The ethical-political import of tragedy, and of the aesthetic in general, resides in the fact that it makes possible individuals who are free in the way Goethe was. Freedom, in the practical sense, consists in wanting and acting in accordance with one's own judgment; it is realized insight into the good. How we can constrain and indeed punch holes in this idea of the self conducted by reasons and purposes (for constrain and punch holes in it we *must*), since it chains the self to its subjectivity, to its social participation) *without becoming unfree,* is the teaching the artists offer, the teaching that constitutes the ethical-political import of the aesthetic. Because it releases us into a different unfolding of our own forces, the aesthetic experience provides a freedom from practical freedom that is not a submission to an overwhelming outside power. The beginning and end of aesthetics is human freedom.

———

* "'Tragedy and the Free Spirits': Considerations on the Ethical-Political Import of Musical Drama" was the working title Nietzsche entered in his notes when he was writing *The Birth of Tragedy* (n. 1).

NOTES

I. SENSIBILITY: THE INDETERMINACY OF THE IMAGINATION

1. Descartes to Mersenne, 18 March 1630, in René Descartes, *Œuvres*, ed. Charles Adam and Paul Tannery, *Correspondance* (Paris: Vrin, 1974–89), 1:132–33. English translation in René Descartes, *Philosophical Letters*, trans. and ed. Anthony Kenny (Minneapolis: University of Minnesota Press, 1970), 7.

2. See Descartes to Princess Elizabeth, May or June 1645, in Descartes, *Correspondance* (n. 1), 4:220; translation in *Philosophical Letters* (n. 1), 162. Cf. the chapter "Le jeu sensible des couleurs," in Pascal Dumont, *Descartes et l'esthétique: L'art d'émerveiller* (Paris: Presses Universitaires de France, 1997), 44–62.

3. Cf. René Descartes, *Compendium of Music*, trans. Walter Robert (n.p.: American Institute of Musicology, 1961). Descartes quotes from this (then unpublished) work in his letter to Mersenne; cf. also the concept of the senses in this text (ibid., 11–13).

4. Cf. Dumont, *Descartes et l'esthétique* (n. 2), 71–102 passim. See also the definition of the "aesthetic regime" in Jacques Rancière, *The Politics of Aesthetics: The Distribution of the Sensible*, trans. Gabriel Rockhill (London: Continuum, 2004), 21–23.

5. *The Philosophical Writings of René Descartes*, trans. John Cottingham, Robert Stoothoff, and Dugald Murdoch, 2 vols. (Cambridge: Cambridge University Press, 1984–85). The following abbreviations refer to Descartes's writings: *Rules = Regulae ad directionem ingenii—Rules for the Direction of the Mind*, 1:7–78; *Discourse = Discours de la méthode pour bien conduire sa raison, et chercher la vérité dans les sciences—Discourse on the Method*, 1:111–51; and *Meditations = Meditationes de prima philosophia—Meditations on First Philosophy*, 2:3–62.

6. Catherine Wilson, "Discourses of Vision in Seventeenth-Century Metaphysics," in *Sites of Vision: The Discursive Construction of Sight in the History of Philosophy*, ed. David Michael Levin (Cambridge, Mass.: MIT Press, 1997), 129. For the following cf. Dennis L. Sepper, *Descartes's Imagination: Proportion, Images, and the Activity of Thinking* (Berkeley: University of California Press, 1996). Sepper examines in great detail the differences with respect to this question among the various phases of Descartes's philosophical thought.

7. But how are we to conceive of something entirely haphazard as being subject to any sort of control? Not, in any case, after the model of political authority, for that is

authority over subjects who exercise self-control. Cf. Georges Canguilhem, "Machine and Organism," in *Knowledge of Life*, trans. Stefanos Geroulanos and Daniela Ginsburg (New York: Fordham University Press, 2008), 86.

8. Descartes to Princess Elizabeth, May or June 1645, in Descartes, *Correspondance* (n. 1), 4:220; translation in *Philosophical Letters* (n. 1), 162.

9. Blaise Pascal, *Pensées*, no. 162, ed. Léon Brunschvicg (Paris: Garnier-Flammarion, 1976); trans. F. W. Trotter, introd. T. S. Eliot (London: Dent; New York: Dutton, 1908), 48. Cf. Erich Köhler, "'Je ne sais quoi.' Ein Kapitel aus der Begriffsgeschichte des Unbegreiflichen," in Köhler, *Esprit und arkadische Freiheit: Aufsätze aus der Welt der Romania* (Frankfurt am Main: Athenäum, 1966), 230–86.

10. Baruch de Spinoza, *Ethics*, in *Complete Works*, trans. Samuel Shirley, ed. Michael L. Morgan (Indianapolis: Hackett, 2002), 213–382, quote in part I, appendix, 240. For a similar description of the tendency to misuse, in the senses, "the order of nature," cf. *Meditations*, VI.15; 57.

11. Thus David E. Wellbery with regard to Wieland: "Die Enden des Menschen: Anthropologie und Einbildungskraft im Bildungsroman bei Wieland, Goethe, Novalis," in Wellbery, *Seiltänzer des Paradoxalen: Aufsätze zur ästhetischen Wissenschaft* (Munich: Hanser, 2006), 77. The "subreption" of the imagination constitutes its "pathology" (ibid., 79).

12. Thus Carsten Zelle, *Die doppelte Ästhetik der Moderne: Revisionen des Schönen von Boileau bis Nietzsche* (Stuttgart: Metzler, 1995), 25ff.

13. Cf. Robert Sommer, *Grundzüge einer Geschichte der deutschen Psychologie und Aesthetik von Wolff-Baumgarten bis Kant-Schiller* (Hildesheim: Olms, 1975), 10ff. and 168ff.; Alfred Baeumler, *Das Irrationalitätsproblem in der Ästhetik und Logik des 18. Jahrhunderts bis zur Kritik der Urteilskraft* (Darmstadt: Wissenschaftliche Buchgesellschaft, 1974), 38–43. Regarding this interpretation of aesthetics based on the difference between Leibniz and Descartes cf. Ernst Cassirer, *Leibniz' System in seinen wissenschaftlichen Grundlagen* (Hildesheim: Olms, 1980), 458–72; Cassirer, *Freiheit und Form: Studien zur deutschen Geistesgeschichte* (Darmstadt: Wissenschaftliche Buchgesellschaft, 1994), 48–66.

14. G. W. Leibniz, *Monadology*, ed. Nicholas Rescher (Pittsburgh: University of Pittsburgh Press, 1991) [= *Monadology*], §11, 68. The notion of a "principle" is already articulated by Pascal with respect to the "esprit de finesse": *Pensées* (n. 9), 1; 1. Regarding the following, cf. Martin Schneider, "Denken und Handeln der Monade: Leibniz' Begründung der Subjektivität," *Studia Leibnitiana* 30(1) (1998): 68–82.

15. "Perceptions are inner activities in the monadic unity of the soul; they arise because the soul is a force; the efforts (*conatus*) contained in this power to pass from one condition to another are appetitions and, accordingly, volitional processes." Wilhelm Dilthey, "The Three Epochs of Modern Aesthetics and Its Present Task" [1892], trans. Michael Neville, in Dilthey, *Selected Works*, vol. 5, *Poetry and Experience*, ed. Rudolf A. Makkreel and Frithjof Rodi (Princeton, N.J.: Princeton University Press, 1985), 182 (translation modified). For the original, see Wilhelm Dilthey, "Die drei

Epochen der modernen Ästhetik und ihre heutige Aufgabe," in Dilthey, *Gesammelte Schriften*, vol. 6 (Leipzig: Teubner, ²1938), 242–87, here 248.

16. Leibniz, *Theodicy*, trans. E. M. Huggard, ed. Austin Farrer (London: Routledge and Kegan Paul, 1951), §§403, 365. Leibniz refers to this passage in his *Monadology* (§23, 98).

17. Gottfried Wilhelm Leibniz, *New Essays on Human Understanding*, trans. and ed. Peter Remnant and Jonathan Bennett (Cambridge: Cambridge University Press, 1996), preface, 53; the following quote, ibid., 54. Regarding the double legibility of this passage cf. Gilles Deleuze, *Difference and Repetition*, trans. Paul Patton (New York: Columbia University Press, 1994), 213–14.

18. I am indebted to four works for important impulses that propelled my considerations in the following sections. Regarding the concept of faculty, see Andrew Kern, *Quellen des Wissens: Zum Begriff vernünftiger Erkenntnisfähigkeiten* (Frankfurt am Main: Suhrkamp, 2006); Matthias Haase, *Conceptual Capacities*, PhD diss., University of Potsdam, 2007. Regarding the difference between forces and faculties, see Thomas Khurana, *Sinn und Gedächtnis: Die Zeitlichkeit des Sinns und die Figuren ihrer Reflexion* (Munich: Fink, 2007); Dirk Setton, *Unvermögen: Irrationalität und der Begriff der rationalen Fähigkeit* (Berlin: Diaphanes, 2011).

2. PRAXIS: THE PRACTICE OF THE SUBJECT

1. Alexander Gottlieb Baumgarten, *Reflections on Poetry—Meditationes philosophicae de nonnullis ad poema pertinentibus*, trans. Karl Aschenbrenner (Berkeley: University of California Press, 1954 [= *Poetry*]).

2. Georg Friedrich Meier, *Anfangsgründe aller schönen Wissenschaften*, §2 (Halle: Hemmerde, ²1754), repr. (Hildesheim: Olms, 1976), 1:3. See also, his substantial criticisms of Baumgarten notwithstanding, Johann Gottfried Herder, *Über die neuere deutsche Literatur: Fragmente, als Beilagen zu den Briefen, die neueste Literatur betreffend. Dritte Sammlung*, in *Werke*, vol. 1 (*Frühe Schriften, 1764–1772*), ed. Ulrich Gaier (Frankfurt am Main: Deutscher Klassiker Verlag, 1985), 397. A translation of selections from *Über die neuere deutsche Literatur* can be found in Johann Gottfried Herder, "On Recent German Literature. Third Collection of Fragments," in *Selected Early Works, 1764–1767*, trans. Ernest A. Menze with Michael Palma, ed. Ernest A. Menze and Karl Menges (University Park: Pennsylvania State University Press, 1992), quote on 198.

3. G. W. Leibniz, "Meditations on Knowledge, Truth, and Ideas" [originally in *Acta eruditorum*, November 1684], in Leibniz, *Philosophical Papers and Letters*, trans. Leroy E. Loemker, 2nd ed. (Dordrecht: Reidel, 1976), 291. Regarding the importance of these considerations to Baumgarten, see Ernst Cassirer, *The Philosophy of the Enlightenment*, trans. F. C. Koelln and J. P. Pettegrove (Princeton, N.J.: Princeton University Press, 1951), 342–43, and Ursula Franke, *Kunst als Erkenntnis: Die Rolle der Sinnlichkeit in der Ästhetik des Alexander Gottlieb Baumgarten* (Wiesbaden:

Steiner, 1972), 44ff. For the following cf. especially Jeffrey Barnouw, "The Beginnings of 'Aesthetics' and the Leibnizian Conception of Sensation," in Paul Mattick, ed., *Eighteenth-Century Aesthetics and the Reconstruction of Art* (Cambridge: Cambridge University Press, 1993), 52–95, here 82ff.

4. Leibniz, "Meditations on Knowledge, Truth, and Ideas" (n. 3), 291.

5. Leibniz, "Meditations on Knowledge, Truth, and Ideas" (n. 3), 292.

6. Alexander Gottlieb Baumgarten, *Aesthetica—Ästhetik*, ed. and German trans. Dagmar Mirbach (Hamburg: Meiner, 2007 [= *Aesthetics*]), §§17 and 1, and cf. §9.

7. Jean de la Bruyère, *Characters*, trans. Henri van Laun (London: Nimmo, 1885), 10. For the history of the concept of taste, see Baeumler, *Das Irrationalitätsproblem* (chap. 1, n. 13), passim; Franz Schümmer, "Die Entwicklung des Geschmacksbegriffs in der Philosophie des 17. und 18. Jahrhunderts," in *Archiv für Begriffsgeschichte* 1 (1955), 120–41.

8. Abbé Du Bos, *Réflexions critiques sur poésie et peinture* [1719] (Paris: Pissot, ⁷1770), repr. (Geneva: Slatkine, 1967), vol. 2, chap. 22, 344 and 343. English: *Critical Reflections on Poetry and Painting*, trans. Thomas Nugent (London: John Nourse, 1748), vol. 2, 240 (translation modified).

9. Baumgarten uses the term "aesthetic truth" in a wider sense: as a cognition of the object in the ordered complexity of its qualities. Cf. p. 25; for a more detailed discussion see Heinz Paetzold, *Ästhetik des deutschen Idealismus: Zur Idee ästhetischer Rationalität bei Baumgarten, Kant, Schelling, Hegel und Schopenhauer* (Wiesbaden: Steiner, 1983), 29ff.

10. Du Bos, *Réflexions critiques* (n. 8), vol. 2, chap. 23, 369–70; English, 258.

11. Ibid., 358; English, 250.

12. David Hume, "Of the Standard of Taste," in Hume, *Essays Moral, Political, and Literary*, ed. Eugene F. Miller (Indianapolis: Liberty Fund, 1985), 226–49; here 235 and 237.

13. See p. 4. Regarding the relation between theory and praxis in Descartes cf. Georges Canguilhem, "Descartes et la technique," *Travaux du XIe congrès international de philosophie: Congrès Descartes*, vol. 2, *Études cartésiennes: IIme partie*, ed. Raymond Bayer (Paris: Hermann, 1937), 77–85. Canguilhem concludes that there is in "Cartesian philosophy no theory of creation, which is to say at bottom, no aesthetics" because of the primacy of theory (ibid., 85).

14. Thus Baumgarten's editor, Hans Rudolf Schweizer, in a note regarding §527 of Baumgarten's *Metaphysics*; see Alexander Gottlieb Baumgarten, *Texte zur Grundlage der Ästhetik*, German trans. and ed. Hans Rudolf Schweizer (Hamburg: Meiner, 1983), 89. The term "subjectivity" thus comes to supplant "taste," as Karl Homann argues in "Zum Begriff 'Subjektivität' bis 1802," in *Archiv für Begriffsgeschichte* 11 (1967), 184–205, here 204–5. Regarding the philosophical-historical context, see Hartmut Scheible, *Wahrheit und Subjekt: Ästhetik im bürgerlichen Zeitalter* (Reinbek bei Hamburg: Rowohlt, 1988), 72–97. Cf. Arbogast Schmitt, "Die Entgrenzung der Künste durch ihre Ästhetisierung bei Baumgarten," in *Ästhetische Erfahrung im Zeichen der Entgrenzung der Künste: Epistemische, ästhetische und religiöse Formen von*

Erfahrung im Vergleich (Zeitschrift für Ästhetik und Allgemeine Kunstwissenschaft), special ed., ed. Gert Mattenklott (Hamburg: Meiner, 2004), 55–71.

15. Cf. Rudolf Rehn, "Subjekt/Prädikat I," in *Historisches Wörterbuch der Philosophie*, vol. 10, ed. Joachim Ritter and Karlfried Gründer (Basel: Schwabe, 1998), cols. 433–37. Regarding the wider—ontological, rhetorical, political—aspects of the meaning of the premodern concept of the subject, see Brigitte Kible, "Subjekt I," ibid., cols. 373–83.

16. In interpreting aesthetics before Kant as a rehash of "humanist"—and ultimately Aristotelian—basic concepts, Hans-Georg Gadamer (see *Truth and Method*, 2nd ed., trans. Joel Weinsheimer and Donald G. Marshall [London: Continuum, 2004], 8–37) disregards the fact that aesthetics is enlightenment and, as a result, also fails to see why, even before Kant, aesthetics needed the concept of the subject. Cf. p. 28.

17. Martin Heidegger, *Nietzsche*, vol. 1, *The Will to Power as Art*, trans. David Farrell Krell (London: Routledge, 1981), and vol. 4, *Nihilism*, trans. Frank A. Capuzzi (San Francisco: Harper and Row, 1982) [= *Nietzsche*].

18. Joachim Ritter, "Landschaft: Zur Funktion des Ästhetischen in der modernen Gesellschaft," in Ritter, *Subjektivität* (Frankfurt am Main: Suhrkamp, 1974), 141–64 [= "Landschaft"]. In the present context, I will limit my summary of Ritter's position, which is paradigmatic for the German discussion, to its subject-theoretical position. Ritter connects it to the larger claim that the aesthetic relation to the world presents the survival under modern conditions of the fundamental structure of ancient *theoria*.

19. Joachim Ritter, "Subjektivität und industrielle Gesellschaft," in Ritter, *Subjektivität* (n. 18), 31. On this point Ritter agrees with Adorno: "[A]rt becomes social by its opposition to society" (Theodor W. Adorno, *Aesthetic Theory*, trans. Robert Hullot-Kentor [Minneapolis: University of Minnesota Press, 1997], 296).

20. Vivid cognition consists in the cognition, based on "something similar, equal, congruent, and in general in a more notable fashion identical," of "another similar, equal, congruent, and in a more notable fashion identical" (*Aesthetics*, §735): Baumgarten's aesthetics is regulated by the model of the metaphor. Regarding the aesthetic concept of vividness cf. Jan Völker, *Ästhetik der Lebendigkeit: Kants dritte Kritik* (Munich: Fink, 2011).

21. Michel Foucault, *Discipline and Punish: The Birth of the Prison*, trans. Alan Sheridan (New York: Vintage, 1979) [= *Discipline*].

22. Michel Foucault, "Une histoire restée muette" [review of Cassirer's *Philosophy of the Enlightenment*], *La quinzaine littéraire* 8 (July 1966): 3–4.

23. Cf. Terry Eagleton, *The Ideology of the Aesthetic* (Oxford: Blackwell, 1990), chap. 1, 13–30. For a detailed examination of the nexus of aesthetics, ethics, and politics in Baumgarten see Howard Caygill, *The Art of Judgment* (Oxford: Blackwell, 1989), 103–88.

3. PLAY: THE OPERATION OF FORCE

1. Herder's German editors group these sketches under the title "Begründung einer Ästhetik in der Auseinandersetzung mit Alexander Gottlieb Baumgarten" ("Foundations for an Aesthetics in Critical Engagement with Alexander Gottlieb Baumgarten") ["Baumgarten"], in Herder, *Werke*, vol. 1, *Frühe Schriften: 1764–1772*, ed. Ulrich Gaier (Frankfurt am Main: Deutscher Klassiker Verlag, 1985), 651–94; quote, 662. Some of these notes are available in English translation: Herder, "A Monument to Baumgarten" ["Monument"], in *Selected Writings on Aesthetics*, trans. Gregory Moore (Princeton, N.J.: Princeton University Press, 2006), 41–50. Cf. Hans Adler, *Die Prägnanz des Dunklen: Gnoseologie—Ästhetik—Geschichtsphilosophie bei Johann Gottfried Herder* (Hamburg: Meiner, 1990), 63–87. Adler reads Herder's concept of the obscure as aiming at a deeper (and simultaneously higher, that is, beautiful) unity with form (as the category of clarity) and draws on Herder's theory of the arts for illustration (ibid., 88–149). Because I am focusing in this chapter on Herder's conception of the obscure as force, I am not considering his theory of arts, which I address in chapter four.

2. Johann Gottfried Herder, "Critical Forests, or Reflections on the Art and Science of the Beautiful: Fourth Grove, On Riedel's *Theory of the Beaux Arts*" ["Fourth Grove"], in *Selected Writings on Aesthetics* (n. 1), 199.

3. Johann Gottfried Herder, "Wie die Philosophie zum Besten des Volks allgemeiner und nützlicher werden kann," in Herder, *Werke*, vol. 1 (n. 1), 132. Cf. Caroline Torra-Mattenklott, *Metaphorologie der Rührung: Ästhetische Theorie und Mechanik im 18. Jahrhundert* (Munich: Fink, 2002), chap. 5, especially 301.

4. Cf. Hans Adler, "Fundus Animae—der Grund der Seele: Zur Gnoseologie des Dunklen in der Aufklärung," *Deutsche Vierteljahrsschrift für Literaturwissenschaft und Geistesgeschichte* 62 (1988): 197–220.

5. Johann Gottfried Herder, *On the Cognition and Sensation of the Human Soul: Observations and Dreams*, in *Philosophical Writings*, trans. Michael N. Forster (Cambridge: Cambridge University Press, 2002 [*Cognition*]), 195 (translation modified).

6. Johann Gottfried Herder, "Versuch über das Sein," in *Werke*, vol. 1 (n. 1), 15.

7. Regarding the structure of Herder's concept of expression see Charles Taylor, *Sources of the Self: The Making of the Modern Identity* (Cambridge, Mass.: Harvard University Press, 1989), 368–90. Taylor interprets that which is expressed not as force but as meaning, reading "force" exclusively in the causal sense of the term; cf. Charles Taylor, "Force et sens," in *Sens et existence: En hommage à Paul Ricœur*, ed. Gary Brent Madison (Paris: Seuil, 1975), 124–37. Rüdiger Campe has shown how the seventeenth and eighteenth centuries gradually "homogenize" "expression" by conceptualizing it as the expression of an utterance and, thus, of an intentional meaning; see Rüdiger Campe, *Affekt und Ausdruck: Zur Umwandlung der literarischen Rede im 17. und 18. Jahrhundert* (Tübingen: Niemeyer, 1990), esp. chap. 2, 184 and 206–7. In light of this observation, Herder's "expressivism" appears to be ambiguous. He, too, relates expression to an act, but he does not conceive of this act in "hermeneutic" terms (ibid., 190).

8. Regarding the various facets of Herder's concept of force, see Robert Clark, "Herder's Conception of 'Kraft,'" in *Publications of the Modern Language Association* 57(3) (1942): 737–52. Cf. Ulrike Zeuch, "'Kraft' als Inbegriff menschlicher Seelentätigkeit in der Anthropologie der Spätaufklärung (Herder und Moritz)," in *Jahrbuch der Schillergesellschaft* 43 (1999), 99–122.

9. Johann Gottfried Herder, "Critical Forests: First Grove, Dedicated to Mr. Lessing's *Laocoön*," in *Selected Writings on Aesthetics* (n. 1), 142. Cf. Torra-Mattenklott, *Metaphorologie der Rührung* (n. 3), 314–15.

10. Gottfried Wilhelm Leibniz, "On the Correction of Metaphysics and the Concept of Substance," in *Philosophical Papers and Letters*, trans. Leroy E. Loemker, vol. 2 (Chicago: University of Chicago Press), 709.

11. For Newton's concept of force, see Richard S. Westfall, "The Culmination of the Scientific Revolution: Isaac Newton," in *Action and Reaction: Proceedings of a Symposium to Commemorate the Tercentenary of Newton's* Principia, ed. Paul Theerman and Adele F. Seeff (Newark: University of Delaware Press, 1993), 37. Alexandre Koyré has shown that Newton himself thought a purely mechanical conception of force insufficient; see *From the Closed World to the Infinite Universe* (Baltimore: Johns Hopkins University Press, 1957), chap. 9.

12. That is why Herder also says of the "spiritual bond" that constitutes life that it "cannot be further explained, but must be *believed* because it *exists*, because it *reveals* itself in a hundred thousand phenomena" (*Cognition*, 192). Here, then, Herder shares Kant's skepticism regarding an objective use of the concept of life. Cf. James L. Larson, "Vital Forces: Regulative Principles or Constitutive Agents? A Strategy in German Physiology, 1786–1802," *Isis* 70 (1979): 235–49, which refers to Johann Friedrich Blumenbach, "Über den Bildungstrieb (Nisus formativus) und seinen Einfluß auf die Generation und Reproduktion," *Göttingisches Magazin der Wissenschaften und Litteratur*, ed. Georg Christoph Lichtenberg and Georg Forster, 1(5) (1780): 247–66.

13. Herder uses the figure of "play" to distinguish the work of forces from the exercise of faculties. By contrast, since Kant and, especially, Schiller, the concept of play has been used to describe *the interrelation between* force and faculty; see also Ruth Sonderegger, *Für eine Ästhetik des Spiels: Hermeneutik, Dekonstruktion und der Eigensinn der Kunst* (Frankfurt am Main: Suhrkamp, 2000), pt. II (with reference to Friedrich Schlegel).

14. Johann Gottfried Herder, "This Too a Philosophy of History for the Formation of Humanity," in *Philosophical Writings* (n. 5), 298.

15. Johann Gottfried Herder, *Ideen zur Philosophie der Geschichte der Menschheit*, 1. Teil, 4. Buch, IV, in Herder, *Werke*, vol. 6, ed. Martin Bollacher (Frankfurt am Main: Deutscher Klassiker Verlag, 1989), 143. Helmuth Plessner quotes this passage in the conclusion of his *Laughing and Crying: A Study of the Limits of Human Behavior*, trans. James Spencer Churchill and Marjorie Grene (Evanston, Ill.: Northwestern University Press, 1970), 157, where he lays out the program of a conjunction of aesthetics and anthropology. This program, he writes, is directed both against an

aesthetics defined by "the prejudice that insists on a dominant role in aesthetics for the concepts of beauty and ugliness" and against the "theory of human behavior," which "has remained hitherto in the shadow of classical philosophy and has taken its guiding principles from the normative sciences." Regarding Plessner's philosophy, see the reconstruction in Hans-Peter Krüger, *Zwischen Lachen und Weinen*, vol. 1, *Das Spektrum menschlicher Phänomene* (Berlin: Akademie, 1999). Regarding the following, cf. also Gerhard Gamm, *Flucht aus der Kategorie: Die Positivierung des Unbestimmten als Ausgang aus der Moderne* (Frankfurt am Main: Suhrkamp, 1994), 73–99, 212–34.

16. Herder, "Versuch über das Sein," in *Werke*, vol. 1 (n. 1), 11. It is consistent with the tendency of his interpretation that Adler (*Die Prägnanz des Dunklen* [n. 1], 54) reads this passage as Herder's "getting serious about the notion of 'man in his entirety.'"

4. AESTHETICIZATION: THE TRANSFORMATION OF PRAXIS

1. Yet Herder describes the materials of this psychophysiological cognition as "[b]iographies, observations of doctors and friends, prophecies of poets—these alone can provide us with material for the true science of the soul" (*Cognition*, 197).

2. Herder, *Über die neuere deutsche Literatur. . . . Dritte Sammlung* (chap. 2, n. 2), 388–89.

3. Herder's thoughts on this point are ambiguous: His concept of the "maternal language," within which the individual's "rights as landlord and owner" are to enjoy unqualified respect (*Über die neuere deutsche Literatur. . . . Dritte Sammlung* [chap. 2, n. 2], 388), effaces this incongruity between the dark mechanism within man and his subjectivity.

4. Plato, *Ion*, in *Plato in Twelve Volumes*, Loeb Classical Library, vol. 8, *The Statesman*, trans. W.R.M. Lamb (Cambridge, Mass.: Harvard University Press, 1925), 533e–534b.

5. Hans-Georg Gadamer, "Plato and the Poets," in *Dialogue and Dialectic: Eight Hermeneutical Studies on Plato*, trans. P. Christopher Smith (New Haven, Conn.: Yale University Press, 1983), 42.

6. Thus (though aiming not at Plato but at Schopenhauer) Friedrich Nietzsche, *On the Genealogy of Morality*, trans. Maudemarie Clark and Alan J. Swensen (Indianapolis: Hackett, 1998), III.5; 72.

7. Regarding the rift within the "aesthetic" this adumbrates, see the section on "Becoming Aesthetic," p. 59.

8. Johann Georg Sulzer, "Von der Kraft (Energie) in den Werken der schönen Künste" [= "Energie"], in Sulzer, *Vermischte philosophische Schriften* (Leipzig: Weidmann und Reich, 1773, repr. Hildesheim: Olms, 1974), 1:122. The quote from Horace translates as "the fire and force of passion" "in language and subject-matter" (Horace, *Satires* I.4, in *Horace: Satires and Epistles. Persius: Satires*, trans. Niall Rudd (Middlesex: Penguin, 1973).

9. Klaus Dockhorn, "Die Rhetorik als Quelle des vorromantischen Irrationalismus in der Literatur- und Geistesgeschichte," in Dockhorn, *Macht und Wirkung der Rheto-*

rik: Vier Aufsätze zur Ideengeschichte der Vormoderne (Bad Homburg: Gehlen, 1968), 94. Regarding the rhetorical theory of *pathos* and its moving force, see ibid., 53–57.

10. Immanuel Kant, *Critique of Judgment*, trans. Werner S. Pluhar (Indianapolis: Hackett, 1987 [= *CJ*]), §14, B43; 72. Cf. the contrary interpretations offered by Konrad Paul Liessmann, *Reiz und Rührung: Über ästhetische Empfindungen* (Vienna: Facultas, 2004), 37–40, and Alenka Zupancic, "Real-Spiel," in *Spieltrieb: Was bringt die Klassik auf die Bühne?* ed. Felix Ensslin (Berlin: Theater der Zeit, 2006), 209–10.

11. "This, then, lends the greatest importance to the liberal arts, that by vividly depicting good and evil they maintain the forces of our soul in a highly advantageous activity; and therein lies the most important force of these arts." Johann Georg Sulzer, s.v. "Kraft," in Sulzer, *Allgemeine Theorie der schönen Künste*, Dritter Theil (Leipzig: Weidemann, ²1793), repr. (Hildesheim: Olms, 1994), 65.

12. Edmund Burke, *A Philosophical Enquiry into the Origin of Our Ideas of the Sublime and Beautiful* [= *Enquiry*], ed. Adam Phillips (Oxford: Oxford University Press, 1990), 122.

13. Moses Mendelssohn, "Rhapsody or additions to the Letters on sentiments" [= "Rhapsody"], in *Philosophical Writings*, trans. Daniel O. Dahlstrom (Cambridge: Cambridge University Press, 1997), 131–68. Regarding the argument of Mendelssohn's essay and its historical context and significance cf. Carsten Zelle, *Angenehmes Grauen: Literaturhistorische Beiträge zur Ästhetik des Schrecklichen im achtzehnten Jahrhundert* (Hamburg: Meiner, 1987), chap. 4.

14. Moses Mendelssohn, "Von dem Vergnügen," in Mendelssohn, *Ästhetische Schriften in Auswahl*, ed. Otto F. Best (Darmstadt: Wissenschaftliche Buchgesellschaft, 1974), 111. "Joy arises from one's opinion that one possesses some good" (René Descartes, *The Passions of the Soul*, trans. Stephen H. Voss [Indianapolis: Hackett, 1989], art. 93, 70).

15. "From the ordinary point of view, the world appears to be something given; from the transcendental point of view, it appears to be something produced (entirely within me). From the aesthetic point of view, the world appears to be given to us just as if we had produced it and to be just the sort of world we would have produced." Johann Gottlieb Fichte, *Foundations of Transcendental Philosophy (Wissenschaftslehre) nova methodo (1796/99)*, ed. and trans. Daniel Breazeale (Ithaca, N.Y.: Cornell University Press, 1992), 473. Regarding Kant's description of the relation between the aesthetic and the philosophical reflection cf. chapter five, this volume, p. 71.

16. Thus Gadamer's description (which is intended as a critique): *Truth and Method* (chap. 2, n. 16), 77–101.

17. This self-transformation is where the "ethical-political" import of the aesthetic resides. See chapter six, this volume, "Ethics."

18. Carl Schmitt, *Politische Romantik* (Berlin: Duncker and Humblot, ³1968), 23; cf. *Political Romanticism*, trans. Guy Oakes (Cambridge, Mass.: MIT Press, 1986), 96. For a metacritique of this critique, see Karl Heinz Bohrer, *Die Kritik der Romantik* (Frankfurt am Main: Suhrkamp, 1989), 284–311. Regarding the problem of the aesthetic object in Kant, see Andrea Kern, *Schöne Lust: Eine Theorie der ästhetischen Erfahrung nach Kant* (Frankfurt am Main: Suhrkamp, 2000), 117–27.

19. Cf. Winfried Menninghaus, "'Darstellung': Friedrich Gottlieb Klopstocks Eröffnung eines neuen Paradigmas," in *Was heißt "Darstellen"?* ed. Christiaan L. Hart Nibbrig (Frankfurt am Main: Suhrkamp, 1994), 205–26. Menninghaus dates this new paradigm to the late 1770s. The writings by Herder, Sulzer, and Mendelssohn discussed here are from the two preceding decades.

20. Friedrich Schiller, *On the Aesthetic Education of Man, in a Series of Letters,* trans. Reginald Snell (New Haven, Conn.: Yale University Press, 1954), 134. Regarding the tension between play (of the "imaginary") and shape (*Gestalt*) cf. Wolfgang Iser, "Von der Gegenwärtigkeit des Ästhetischen," in *Dimensionen ästhetischer Erfahrung,* ed. Joachim Küpper and Christoph Menke (Frankfurt am Main: Suhrkamp, 2003), 176–202. But cf. regarding the interrelation of object and play Martin Seel, *Ästhetik des Erscheinens* (Munich: Hanser, 2000), 70–99.

21. Friedrich Schlegel, "Athenaeum Fragments," fragment no. 238, in Schlegel, *Philosophical Fragments,* trans. Peter Firchow (Minneapolis: University of Minnesota Press, 1991), 51.

5. AESTHETICS: PHILOSOPHY'S CONTENTION

1. Cf. Jean-François Lyotard, *Lessons on the Analytic of the Sublime: Kant's Critique of Judgment,* §§23–29, trans. Elizabeth Rottenberg (Stanford: Stanford University Press, 1994), 67. The surreptitious transition from the "enlivenment" of the cognitive forces to their being in "harmony" (in *CJ,* §9) corresponds to the (equally surreptitious) union of "freedom" and "law" (in *CJ,* §35). Cf. Rodolphe Gasché, *The Idea of Form: Rethinking Kant's Aesthetics* (Stanford: Stanford University Press, 2003), 42–59.

2. Thus the central argument in Kern, *Schöne Lust* (chap. 4, n. 18), 296–309. Paul de Man has analyzed this description of the aesthetic as a medium of self-assurance as "aesthetic ideology"; cf. Paul de Man, *Aesthetic Ideology* (Minneapolis: University of Minnesota Press, 1996), 70–118. Cf. Jens Szczepanski, *Subjektivität und Ästhetik: Gegendiskurse zur Metaphysik des Subjekts im ästhetischen Denken bei Schlegel, Nietzsche und de Man* (Bielefeld: Transcript, 2007), chap. 3.

3. Eric A. Havelock, *Preface to Plato* (Cambridge, Mass.: Belknap, 1963), chaps. I and II; Heinz Schlaffer, *Poesie und Wissen: Die Entstehung des ästhetischen Bewußtseins und der philologischen Erkenntnis* (Frankfurt am Main: Suhrkamp, 1990), pt. I.

4. Xenophanes of Colophon, *Fragments,* trans. J. H. Lesher (Toronto: University of Toronto Press, 1992), fragments 10 and 18.

5. Cf. Hans Blumenberg, "Der Sturz des Protophilosophen—Zur Komik der reinen Theorie, anhand einer Rezeptionsgeschichte der Thales-Anekdote," in *Das Komische,* ed. Wolfgang Preisendanz and Rainer Warning (Munich: Fink, 1976), 11–64.

6. Friedrich Schlegel, "Critical Fragments [from *Lyceum*]," fragment no. 108, in Schlegel, *Philosophical Fragments* (chap. 4, n. 21), 13. Schlegel explains the idea of Socratic irony, but he describes it (here) according to the model of aesthetic irony. Regarding the following cf. p. 36.

7. This complication of the category of possibility has prompted proposals to replace it with terms such as "virtuality" (Gilles Deleuze) or "potentiality" (Giorgio Agamben). My choice of terms draws on Jacques Derrida, "Signature Event Context," trans. Samuel Weber and Jeffrey Mehlman, in Derrida, *Limited Inc* (Evanston, Ill.: Northwestern University Press), 20. The same idea in Derrida (that the condition of possibility must at once also be conceived as that of impossibility) has also inspired a "rhetorical" reading of aesthetics. Like the genealogical reading, it "deconstructs" the philosophical explanation of the practical success of practical faculties. Unlike the genealogical reading, however, it interprets aesthetics—Baumgarten's *Aesthetics*—as a reflection not on an original dark force, which is repressed by practical faculties *and* continues to work, but on concealed "figures of form" (Campe), which, by virtue of their "latency" (Haverkamp), produce effects of success. See Rüdiger Campe, "Bella Evidentia: Begriff und Figur von Evidenz in Baumgartens Ästhetik," in *Deutsche Zeitschrift für Philosophie* 49 (2001): 243–55; Campe, "Der Effekt der Form: Baumgartens Ästhetik am Rande der Metaphysik," in *Literatur als Philosophie—Philosophie als Literatur*, ed. Eva Horn, Bettine Menke, and Christoph Menke (Munich: Fink, 2005), 17–34; Anselm Haverkamp, *Figura cryptica: Theorie der literarischen Latenz* (Frankfurt am Main: Suhrkamp, 2002), 23–43, 73–88; Haverkamp, *Metapher: Die Ästhetik in der Rhetorik* (Munich: Fink, 2007, 42–52). This raises the question of the relation between (aesthetic) force and (rhetorical) figure. It is the hypothesis of aesthetic genealogy that figure is an (expressive) effect of force.

8. Cf. the exemplary examinations of the concepts of meaning in Khurana, *Sinn und Gedächtnis* (chap. 1, n. 18), and of the will in Setton, *Unvermögen—Akrasia—Infantia* (chap. 1, n. 18).

6. ETHICS: THE FREEDOM OF SELF-CREATION

1. Friedrich Nietzsche, *Nachgelassene Fragmente*, September 1870–January 1871, 5[22], in *Kritische Studienausgabe*, ed. Giorgio Colli and Mazzino Montinari (Munich: Deutscher Taschenbuch Verlag and de Gruyter, 1988), 7:97. Quotations from Nietzsche's writings are indicated by the following abbreviations: *BT* = *The Birth of Tragedy and Other Writings*, trans. Speirs (Cambridge: Cambridge University Press, 1999); *GS* = *The Gay Science: With a Prelude in German Rhymes and an Appendix of Songs*, trans. Josefine Nauckhoff (Cambridge: Cambridge University Press, 2001); *TI* = *Twilight of the Idols: Or How to Philosophize with a Hammer*, trans. Duncan Large (Oxford: Oxford University Press, 1998), within which *RRUM* = "Reconnaissance Raids of an Untimely Man"; *Daybreak* = *Daybreak: Thoughts on the Prejudices of Morality*, trans. R. J. Hollingdale (Cambridge: Cambridge University Press, 1997); *BGE* = *Beyond Good and Evil: Prelude to a Philosophy of the Future*, trans. Judith Norman (Cambridge: Cambridge University Press, 2002). The *Nachgelassene Fragmente* of early 1880, in *Kritische Studienausgabe*, 9:9–33 [= *Fragments, 1880*], are not available in English translation.

2. Friedrich Nietzsche, *Unpublished Writings from the Period of the Unfashionable Observations*, trans. Richard T. Gray (Stanford: Stanford University Press, 1995), 19[30]; 11.

3. Cf. *BT* 12, 61–62; and Friedrich Nietzsche, "The Case of Wagner: A Musician's Problem," 5–8, in Nietzsche, *The Anti-Christ, Ecce Homo, Twilight of the Idols, and Other Writings*, trans. Judith Norman (Cambridge: Cambridge University Press, 2005), 240–49.

4. Cf. *BT* 4, 26: "reduction [*Depotenziren*] of semblance to semblance." Cf. Karl Heinz Bohrer, "Ästhetik und Historismus: Nietzsches Begriff des 'Scheins,'" in Bohrer, *Plötzlichkeit: Zum Augenblick des ästhetischen Scheins* (Frankfurt am Main: Suhrkamp, 1981), 111–38. Cf. also Paul de Man, "Rhetoric of Tropes (Nietzsche)," in *Allegories of Reading: Figural Language in Rousseau, Nietzsche, Rilke, and Proust* (New Haven, Conn.: Yale University Press, 1979), 103–18; David E. Wellbery, "Form und Funktion der Tragödie nach Nietzsche," in *Tragödie—Trauerspiel—Spektakel*, ed. Bettine Menke and Christoph Menke (Berlin: Theater der Zeit, 2007), 199–212.

5. Friedrich Nietzsche, "The Dionysiac World View," 3, in *BT*, 130. This makes a distinction between artistic intoxication and the intoxication in which the "decadent" seek refuge from life: cf. *Daybreak*, 50; 32–33 and *GS*, 370; 234. For the difference between the Dionysian artist and the Dionysian Barbarian, see Peter Sloterdijk, *Der Denker auf der Bühne: Nietzsches Materialismus* (Frankfurt am Main: Suhrkamp, 1986), 59–71.

6. "I do not know what I do when I begin to sing, for I do not *know* that I *can* sing." And "perhaps, then, that singer is most faithful to his destiny who has the capability of passivity, of inaction or equanimity, an ability of inability." Alexander García Düttmann, *Kunstende: Drei ästhetische Studien* (Frankfurt am Main: Suhrkamp, 2000), 25 and 27.

7. Regarding Nietzsche's critique of morality as a critique of its models of action and the agent, see Bernard Williams, "Nietzsche's Minimalist Moral Psychology," in Williams, *Making Sense of Humanity* (Cambridge: Cambridge University Press, 1995), 65–76. "Morality" designates in Nietzsche a mode of subjectivation in the sense proposed by Michel Foucault in *The History of Sexuality*, vol. 2, *The Use of Pleasure*, trans. Robert Hurley (New York: Pantheon, 1985), 25–32. Cf. Martin Saar, *Genealogie als Kritik: Geschichte und Theorie des Subjekts nach Nietzsche und Foucault* (Frankfurt am Main: Campus, 2007).

8. Regarding the following, see Nietzsche, *On the Genealogy of Morality* (chap. 4, n. 6), I.13; 25–26. Cf. also *Daybreak*, 115–16; 71–73, and *TI*, "'Reason' in Philosophy," 5; 18–19.

9. Cf. Robert Pippin, "Lightning and Flash, Agent and Deed" (I, 6–17), in *Friedrich Nietzsche: Zur Genealogie der Moral*, ed. Otfried Höffe (Berlin: Akademie, 2004), 47–64.

10. Cf. Hans Joas, *The Creativity of Action*, trans. Jeremy Gaines and Paul Keast (Cambridge: Polity, 1996), 148–67. For Nietzsche's concept of life, cf. Dieter

Thomä, "Eine Philosophie des Lebens jenseits des Biologismus und diesseits der 'Geschichte der Metaphysik': Bemerkungen zu Nietzsche und Heidegger mit Seitenblicken auf Emerson, Musil und Cavell," in *Heidegger-Jahrbuch* 2:265–96, especially 279.

11. Cf. Martin Seel, *Versuch über die Form des Glücks* (Frankfurt am Main: Suhrkamp, 1995), 87ff.

12. Friedrich Nietzsche, *Morgenröthe*, 9, in *Kritische Studienausgabe* (n. 1), 3:21. Cf. *Daybreak*, 9; 10.

13. Ernst Tugendhat, *Vorlesungen über Ethik* (Frankfurt am Main: Suhrkamp, 1993), 56.

14. I emphasize the argument also against Nietzsche's own experimentation with the idea that to create oneself means to give one's life the unity of a work of beauty. Nietzsche speaks, for example, of the "spectacle of that strength which employs genius *not for works* but for *itself as a work*" (*Daybreak*, 548; 220) and calls "'giving style' to one's character—a great and rare art" (*GS*, 290; 163). Yet the goal of "unity" ties life back to social criteria, depriving it of its aesthetic freedom. For more about the political consequences of aesthetic freedom (an issue Nietzsche addresses) see p. 81 and the pointers in Juliane Rebentisch, "Demokratie und Theater," in *Spieltrieb* (chap. 4, n. 10), 71–81.

15. Cf. chapter four, this volume, p. 59, about the process of aestheticization. To bear—not to undo—the rift between force and faculty in artistic creation is what engenders *"great style"* (*RRUM*, 11, 49). Cf. Karl Heinz Bohrer, "Die Stile des Dionysos," in Bohrer, *Großer Stil: Form und Formlosigkeit in der Moderne* (Munich: Hanser, 2007), 216–35.